Under the Sea

The Nature Company Discoveries Library published by Time-Life Books

Conceived and produced by
Weldon Owen Pty Limited
59 Victoria Street, McMahons Point,
NSW, 2060, Australia
A member of the
Weldon Owen Group of Companies
Sydney • San Francisco
Copyright © 1995 US Weldon Owen Inc.
Copyright © 1995 Weldon Owen Pty Limited
Reprinted 1996 (three times), 1997 (four times),
1999

THE NATURE COMPANY
Priscilla Wrubel, Steve Manning, Tracy Fortini

TIME-LIFE BOOKS
Time-Life Books is a division of Time Life Inc.
Time-Life is a trademark of Time Warner Inc.
U.S.A.

Time-Life Custom Publishing
Vice President and Publisher: Terry Newell
Director of Aquisitions: Jennifer L. Pearce
Managing Editor: Donia Ann Steele
Vice President of Sales and Marketing: Neil Levin
Director of Financial Operations: J. Brian Birky

WELDON OWEN Pty Limited
Chairman: John Owen
Publisher: Sheena Coupe
Managing Editor: Rosemary McDonald
Project Editor: Helen Cooney
Text Editor: Claire Craig
Educational Consultants: Richard L. Needham,
Deborah A. Powell
Art Director: Sue Burk
Designers: Sylvie Abecassis, Michéle
Lichtenberger, Giulietta Pellascio
Assistant Designers: Janet Marando,
Kylie Mulquin
Photo Research Coordinator: Esther Beaton
Photo Research: Karen Burgess,
Amanda Parsonage

Illustrations Research Coordinator: Kathy Gerrard
Production Manager: Caroline Webber
Production Assistant: Kylie Lawson
Vice President, International Sales:
Stuart Laurence

Text: Linsay Knight

Illustrators: Graham Back; Greg Bridges;
Simone End; Christer Eriksson; Mike Golding;
Mike Gorman; Richard Hook/Bernard Thornton
Artists, UK; David Kirshner; Alex Lavroff;
Colin Newman/Garden Studio; Oliver Rennert;
Ken Rinkel; Trevor Ruth; Rod Scott; Steve
Seymour/Bernard Thornton Artists, UK; Ray Sim;
Kevin Stead; Rod Westblade

Library of Congress
Cataloging-in-Publication Data
Under the sea / consulting editor,
Frank H. Talbot.

    p. cm. -- (Discoveries Library)

    Includes index.
    ISBN 0-7835-4760-9

    1. Ocean--Juvenile literature. [1. Ocean.
    2. Marine biology.] I. Talbot, Frank.
    II. Series: Discoveries Library
    (Alexandria, Va.)

    GC21.5.U53 1995
    551.46--dc20   95-12948

Printed by Toppan Printing

A Weldon Owen Production

Under the Sea

CONSULTING EDITOR

Dr. Frank H. Talbot

Director Emeritus, National Museum of Natural History
Smithsonian Institution, Washington DC, USA

TIME
LIFE
BOOKS

Contents

Our Oceans

If you looked at the Earth from space, it would look extremely blue. This is because vast oceans cover almost two-thirds of our "blue planet." The Pacific, the Atlantic, the Indian, the Arctic and the Southern are the world's major oceans. They were formed by complex geological processes that continue to affect the Earth. The Earth is made up of seven main parts, called lithospheric plates, formed from the upper part of the Earth's mantle layer and the crust. Many millions of years ago, these parts all fit together. But nothing on Earth is fixed, and these plates are constantly moving (at about the same speed your fingernails grow) over a layer of soft, squishy rock called the asthenosphere that lies beneath the crust. When two plates move away from each other, hot melted rock, or magma, rises to fill the space and forms a new sea floor. In this way, ocean basins can grow gradually over millions of years. Five million years ago, the Red Sea was a shallow basin. Now, as the sea floor spreads, scientists think it has the makings of a new ocean.

THE BEGINNING
About 250 million years ago, there was one huge continent known as Pangaea, but before this, the real "beginning" is still shrouded in mystery.

PLATES MOVE APART
About 200 to 130 million years ago, Pangaea broke into separate pieces.

DID YOU KNOW?

Alfred Lothar Wegener, who lived between 1880 and 1930, was a German scientist. He was the first to suggest that many millions of years ago the world was one huge supercontinent.

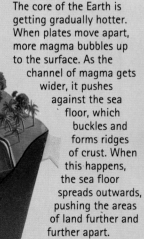

Forces below
The core of the Earth is getting gradually hotter. When plates move apart, more magma bubbles up to the surface. As the channel of magma gets wider, it pushes against the sea floor, which buckles and forms ridges of crust. When this happens, the sea floor spreads outwards, pushing the areas of land further and further apart.

RED SEA SPREADING

The African and Arabian plates began moving apart between five and ten million years ago. As this movement continues at a rate of about $1/2$ in (1 cm) a year, the basin of the Red Sea is spreading slowly. Astronaut Eugene Cernan photographed Africa and the Arabian Peninsula as *Apollo 17* traveled toward the moon in 1972. The gash you can see in the continental crust is called the Great Rift Valley. It runs from the Jordan Valley and Dead Sea in the north down through East Africa in the south, and was probably caused by the movement of the plates.

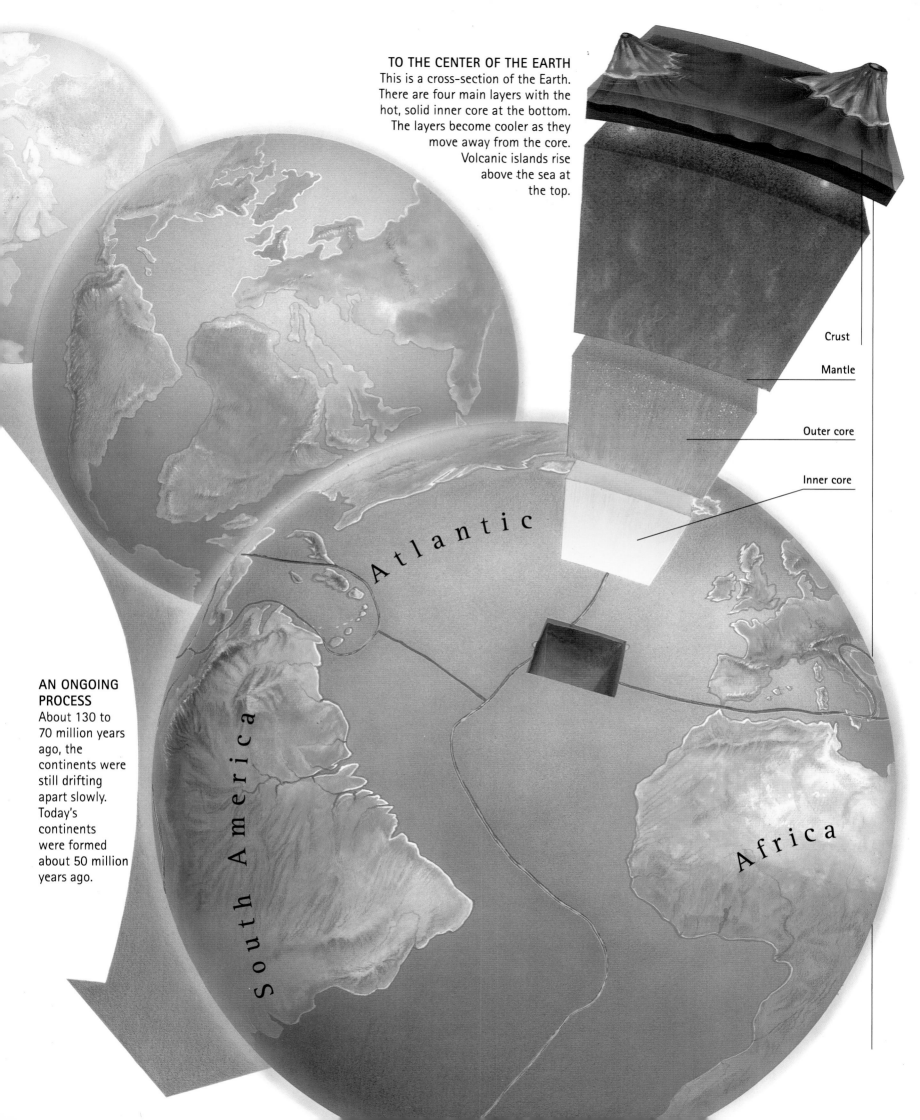

TO THE CENTER OF THE EARTH
This is a cross-section of the Earth. There are four main layers with the hot, solid inner core at the bottom. The layers become cooler as they move away from the core. Volcanic islands rise above the sea at the top.

Crust

Mantle

Outer core

Inner core

Atlantic

South America

Africa

AN ONGOING PROCESS
About 130 to 70 million years ago, the continents were still drifting apart slowly. Today's continents were formed about 50 million years ago.

The Sea Floor

If all the water in the world's oceans was sucked away, we would be able to see the amazing landscape of the sea floor. With huge mountains and deep valleys, slopes and plains, trenches and ridges, it is surprisingly similar to the landscape of dry land. Modern ships and equipment have made it possible for us to learn about this hidden area. Between 1968 and 1975, the deep-sea drilling ship *Glomar Challenge* bored more than 400 holes in the sea bed and collected rock samples to be examined. These helped scientists piece together an accurate picture of the sea floor. They were able to detail its many features, such as a shallow continental shelf that extends from the land into the sea and may once have been dry land; and a continental slope, where the continent ends and the underwater land plunges to the very depths of the sea floor. Scientists continue to chart more of this underwater land with the help of computer images of underwater land forms and maps of the sea bed.

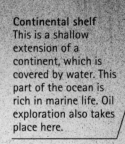

Continental shelf
This is a shallow extension of a continent, which is covered by water. This part of the ocean is rich in marine life. Oil exploration also takes place here.

Continental slope
This is the gently sloping, submerged land near the coast that forms the side of an ocean basin.

VOYAGE TO THE DEEP
This diver looks like an underwater astronaut as he dangles from a line attached to a vessel above.

LAYING CABLE
A diver and an underwater cable layer install telephone cables on the continental shelf.

RESEARCH INSTRUMENTS
Scientists collect and analyze deep-sea specimens and other information from the ocean floor to learn how the underwater landscape was formed. They use instruments such as the bathythermograph, which measures underwater temperatures, and the fisher scoop, which gathers up small samples of sand and mud from the sea bed.

Fisher scoop

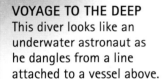

Bathythermograph

PILLOW LAVA
When hot gases and liquid bubble up to the surface of the ocean floor, they harden and turn into lava. This is pillow lava, which has become part of the sea bed near the Galapagos Islands.

Seamounts
Most of these underwater volcanoes remain beneath the sea. Those that rise above the surface form islands.

Guyots
These are flat-topped seamounts.

SEEING WITH SOUND

This map of the sea bed of the Great Barrier Reef in Australia shows a 19-mile (30-km) wide section of the seaward slope. It was produced by GLORIA, a mapping instrument that sends waves of sound energy down to the sea floor and records the returning echoes.

GLORIA
This instrument is attached to its "mother" ship by a conducting cable. It can reach depths of 164 ft (50 m) below the surface.

Abyssal plains
These are some of the flattest places on Earth. They spread out from the oceanic ridge to the edges of the continents.

Oceanic ridge
This is a ridge that rises when new sea floor wells up from inside the Earth.

Oceanic trench
A long, narrow valley, or trench, usually forms next to islands or beside coastal mountain ranges.

DID YOU KNOW?
Some of the world's deepest sea trenches extend further downwards than the highest mountains on land rise upwards.

Sea Upheavals

The ocean is always moving. Its surface can change from calm and mirrorlike to wild and treacherous. Most waves at sea are caused by wind. The waves created by the gales that blow during a tropical cyclone are 46 ft (14 m) and higher. The largest wave known to have been caused by the wind was 112 ft (34 m) high. Waves can also be created by volcanic eruptions or earthquakes under the sea. These waves are known as tsunamis (pronounced soo-nah-mees). They are wide columns of water that reach down to the sea floor and can travel for great distances, at the speed of a jet plane, across the ocean. The surface of the ocean can also be changed by colliding currents. When the tide turns, the opposing currents meet and may create a whirlpool. One famous whirlpool is the fearsome Maelstrom off the coast of Norway. The thunder of its crashing eddies of water can be heard 3 miles (5 km) away.

WHIRLING WINDS

A waterspout is a whirling column of air, laden with mist and spray. First cousin to the tornado, it can occur when rising warm, moist air meets cold, dry air. Sometimes schools of fish are sucked up by the fury of the spout, which can reach nearly 4 miles (6 km) into the air. Waterspouts rarely last more than 60 minutes, and while they are spectacular, they seldom cause any serious damage.

WALL OF WATER

People who live in coastal cities can be affected by sea upheavals. Imagine how frightening it would be to see an enormous wall of water rushing toward you. Your first reaction would be to run, but to where? The impact of the wave could destroy your whole city. Thousands of years ago a large part of Mauna Loa, one of the volcanic Hawaiian Islands, collapsed into the sea. This landslide produced a tsunami that traveled to the next island, Lanai, and crashed across it to a height of 918 feet (280 m). If such an event occurred today, all coastal areas in the Hawaiian Islands would be damaged. Waves of up to 98 ft (30 m) could roll into the city of Honolulu.

A DEVASTATING FORCE

A hurricane has a wind of force 12 or above on the Beaufort Scale, and it may be 400 miles (645 km) wide. This photograph of a hurricane called Elena was taken from the Space Shuttle *Discovery*.

THE BEAUFORT SCALE

This scale uses the numbers 1 to 12 to indicate the strength of wind at sea. At 0, the sea is as calm as a mirror; at 6 there is a strong breeze and large waves 10 ft (3 m) high. At 12, a hurricane is raging and the waves are more than 46 ft (14 m) high.

STORMING AWAY

This dramatically colored image of a severe storm in the Bering Sea was taken from a satellite in space.

Force 2

Force 8

Force 12

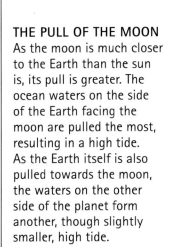

Currents and Tides

Ocean currents are the massive bodies of water that travel long distances around the world. The major force that produces the currents is the wind. There are seven main ocean currents and thousands of smaller ones. They move in large, circular streams at about walking pace (1–5 knots). In the Northern Hemisphere, currents move in a clockwise direction; in the Southern Hemisphere they are counterclockwise. Winds carry the warm or cold water currents along the shorelines, affecting the climate of the various continents on the way. The Gulf Stream, for example, is a current that carries warm water from the Caribbean Sea, up the east coast of the United States and then to the west coasts of Britain and Northern Europe. Without the Gulf Stream, these areas would be much colder. Oceans are also influenced by the "pull" of the moon and the sun. This pull causes the tides. Each day the level of the sea rises and falls and then rises and falls again. Each high tide and the following low tide are about six hours apart. The difference in height between high tide and low tide is called the tidal range. The largest tidal ranges are found in bays and estuaries. The Bay of Fundy in Canada has a tidal range of 49 ft (15 m), the highest in the world. On open coasts the tidal range is usually 6–10 feet (2–3 m).

THE PULL OF THE MOON
As the moon is much closer to the Earth than the sun is, its pull is greater. The ocean waters on the side of the Earth facing the moon are pulled the most, resulting in a high tide. As the Earth itself is also pulled towards the moon, the waters on the other side of the planet form another, though slightly smaller, high tide.

SPRING AND NEAP TIDES

The highest and lowest tides occur when the Earth, the moon and the sun are in line with each other. These tides are called spring tides. When the sun and the moon form a right angle with the Earth, their combined pull is weakest and the difference between high and low tide, the tidal range, is at its lowest. These tides are called neap tides. Spring and neap tides occur twice a month.

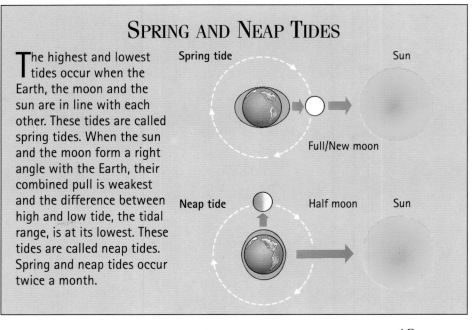

Spring tide

Full/New moon

Sun

Neap tide

Half moon

Sun

IN FAR-FLUNG CORNERS
In 1977, Nigel Wace threw 20 wine bottles overboard from a ship traveling between South America and Antarctica to try to discover how far and how fast ocean litter travels. Most of the bottles took two years to drift to Western Australia and nearly three years to reach New Zealand. Others reached southern Africa, the Seychelles and Easter Island. Because there is so much litter in the oceans, Wace says that today he would not throw any trash into the sea, even for the sake of an experiment.

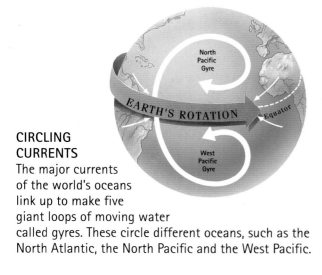

CIRCLING CURRENTS

The major currents of the world's oceans link up to make five giant loops of moving water called gyres. These circle different oceans, such as the North Atlantic, the North Pacific and the West Pacific.

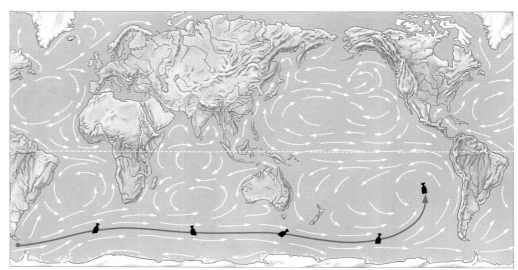

MOVING OCEAN CURRENTS

In the tropics, strong winds push currents towards the equator. In the northern and southern seas, westerly winds push currents eastward. When they reach a continent, they change direction. The spin of the Earth also influences the direction of the currents: those in the northern part of the world are pushed to the right, while those in the southern part are pushed to the left. This phenomenon is called the Coriolis effect.

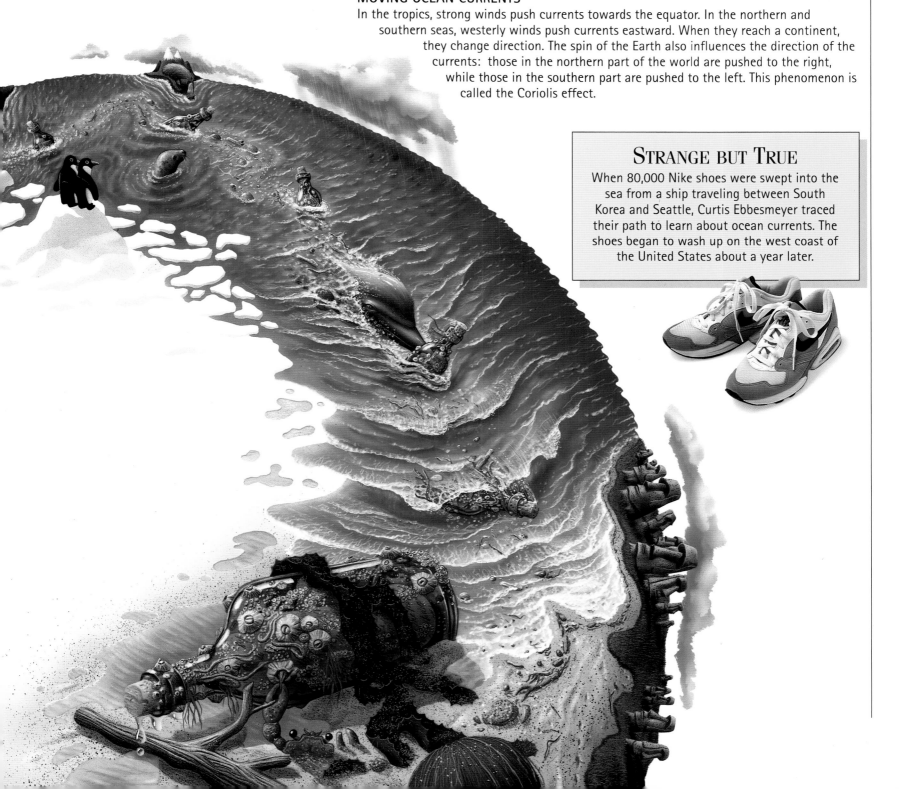

STRANGE BUT TRUE

When 80,000 Nike shoes were swept into the sea from a ship traveling between South Korea and Seattle, Curtis Ebbesmeyer traced their path to learn about ocean currents. The shoes began to wash up on the west coast of the United States about a year later.

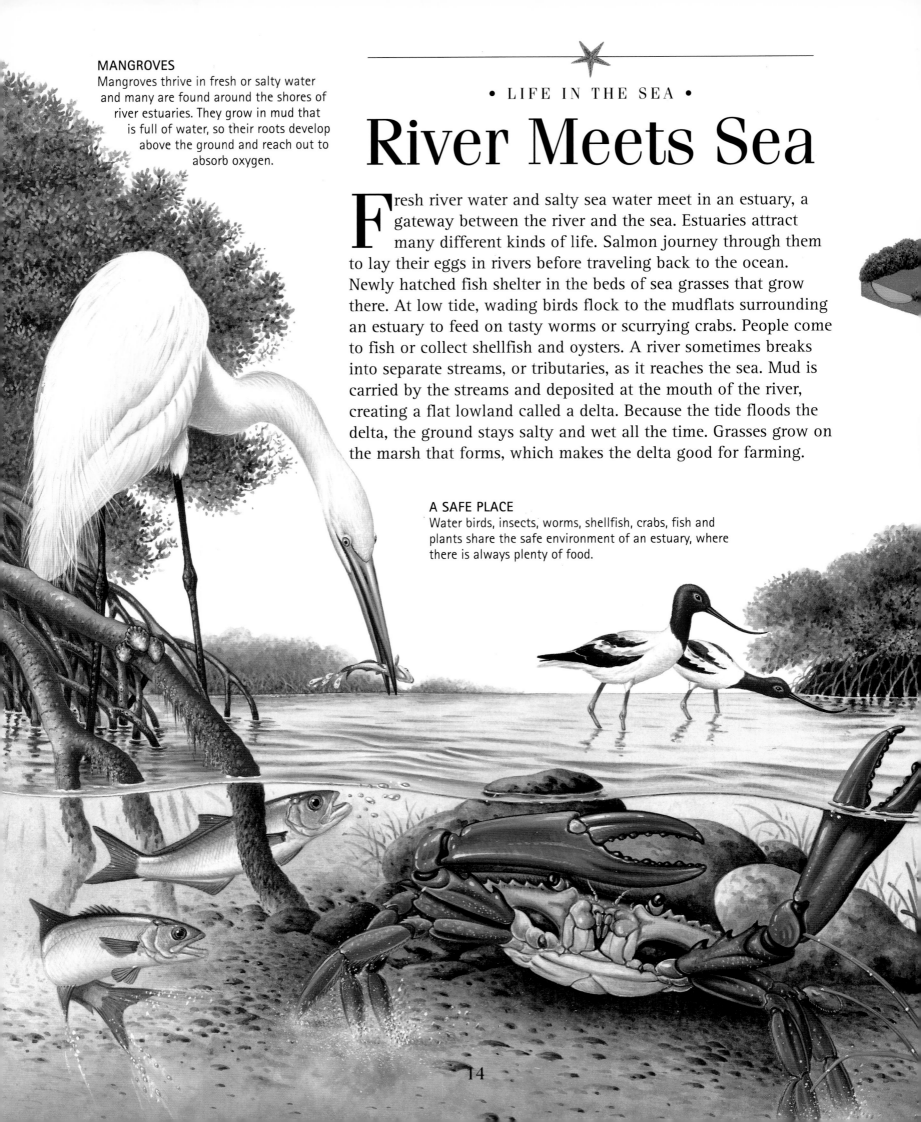

MANGROVES
Mangroves thrive in fresh or salty water and many are found around the shores of river estuaries. They grow in mud that is full of water, so their roots develop above the ground and reach out to absorb oxygen.

River Meets Sea

Fresh river water and salty sea water meet in an estuary, a gateway between the river and the sea. Estuaries attract many different kinds of life. Salmon journey through them to lay their eggs in rivers before traveling back to the ocean. Newly hatched fish shelter in the beds of sea grasses that grow there. At low tide, wading birds flock to the mudflats surrounding an estuary to feed on tasty worms or scurrying crabs. People come to fish or collect shellfish and oysters. A river sometimes breaks into separate streams, or tributaries, as it reaches the sea. Mud is carried by the streams and deposited at the mouth of the river, creating a flat lowland called a delta. Because the tide floods the delta, the ground stays salty and wet all the time. Grasses grow on the marsh that forms, which makes the delta good for farming.

A SAFE PLACE
Water birds, insects, worms, shellfish, crabs, fish and plants share the safe environment of an estuary, where there is always plenty of food.

A VIEW FROM ABOVE

Fresh water from a river flows into a sheltered estuary, where it mixes with salt water from the sea.

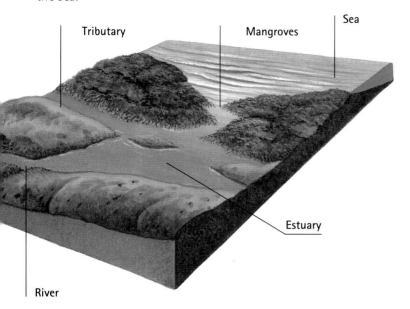

Tributary

Mangroves

Sea

Estuary

River

THE LIFE CYCLE OF A MUSSEL

Mussels begin life as larvae that swim about freely. Tiny, hairlike projections help them move in the water. As mussels grow, they develop a wedge-shaped bivalve shell, which has two sections hinged together. The shells are anchored to rocks by strands, though some species burrow into sand.

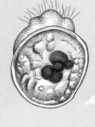

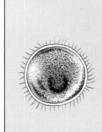

Early larva

Developing larva

Adult mussel

ARCHERFISH
These fish shoot insects with water. When the insects land in the water, the fish are ready to eat them.

CLAMS
Many kinds of clams can be eaten, but you may have difficulty finding these burrowing mollusks.

BLUEFISH
These bluefish are sometimes called tailor because their teeth cut like tailors' scissors. The young are often caught in estuaries by people who like to fish for sport.

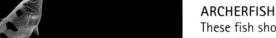

MUD WHELKS
Mud whelks have large, spiral-shaped shells and are related to common garden snails.

GHOST NIPPERS
These small pinkish-white creatures burrow in the muddy sands and nip anyone who tries to catch them.

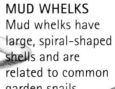

SEA HORSES
These unlikely looking fish swim upright, propelled by dorsal fins.

The Seashore

The land meets the sea at the seashore, which is the home of many animals. Hundreds of species of crabs patrol sandy seashores and hide in rockpools, searching for scraps of food. Crustaceans or mollusks have shells or other hard casing to protect them from birds, the hot sun and the pounding waves. Sand hoppers feed on rotting plants, especially seaweed that has been washed up onto the beach. Sea urchins graze on tiny animals and plants from rocks, and starfish feed on coral and shellfish. Certain corals provide a safe shelter for other seashore animals. Some fish have also adapted to life near the shore. The weeverfish hides in the sand, ready to eat any small fish or crabs that swim nearby. Razor clams and burrowing sea anemones disappear into the sand when they have caught their prey.

Drawn in
Anemones are anchored in one place by their stalks. Their tentacles shorten when fish swim into them and pull the prey into the open mouth of the anemone.

INSIDE A STARFISH

The round center of a starfish body holds the stomach. The anus is above the stomach and the mouth is below. Canals holding water, branches of nerves and intestines spread into each of the five arms. If an arm is broken off, a starfish can grow a new one in a few weeks. A starfish has tubes inside its body that pump water in and out of its many tube feet. As the water pressure builds up, the feet become longer and they bend. This action propels the starfish along. Each tube foot has a little sucker on the end, which the starfish uses to climb rocks and to open shellfish.

Water enters here

Tubes pumping water

Tube feet

Garibaldi
Bright orange male garibaldi seek out small crevices or overhangs in their rock-reef homes. Female garibaldi spawn with males that hold the best nest sites.

Acorn barnacles
The rocky seashore is home to many acorn barnacles. They can feed only when the tide comes in and they are submerged.

Sea otters
These live on the shores of the northern Pacific Ocean. Sea otters use their sharp teeth and strong front paws to crack open the hard shells of crabs.

Kelp
This is a type of large, brown seaweed. It provides food and shelter for all kinds of sea creatures.

Periwinkles
These rough periwinkles can be found just below the waves on rocky shores.

Mulberry whelk
This feeds on dead or dying animals.

Octopus
This has sharp eyesight and a large brain.

Sea urchins
These use their long, sharp spines to defend themselves. Sometimes these spines contain a painful venom.

Suit of armor
The chiton's shell has eight plates that fit one against the other.

Coastal Seas

The coastal seas are the richest areas of the ocean. They teem with sea life and are very popular for fishing and trawling. Most of the fish and shellfish we eat are caught in these shallow waters, which are down to 200 ft (60 m) deep. They spread out over the outer parts of continents and larger islands. Coastal sea water is alive with plankton, tiny drifting plants and animals. When blue and yellow light waves bounce back off this plankton, it makes the water look very green. Fast-swimming fish, such as yellowtails, bluefish, striped bass and some types of tuna, feed off smaller mackerels, sardines and herrings close to the coasts. Humpback whales give birth in warm coastal seas, then push their newborn calves to the surface for their first breath.

NAUTICAL NAUTILUS
The pearly nautilus lives in a shell that has chambers. It controls the gas and fluid in these chambers to keep afloat.

Shell chamber

Gonads

Eye

Beak

Tentacles

Funnel

Gills

PAPER NAUTILUS EGGS
The paper nautilus has a temporary but very beautiful shell, which the female creates to hold her eggs. The eggs shown here have been released from their paper thin and transparent case.

SEA SNAKES
This striking sea snake has a paddle-shaped tail to help it swim quickly through the water. It also has scales on its belly so that it can crawl around on land to mate and lay eggs.

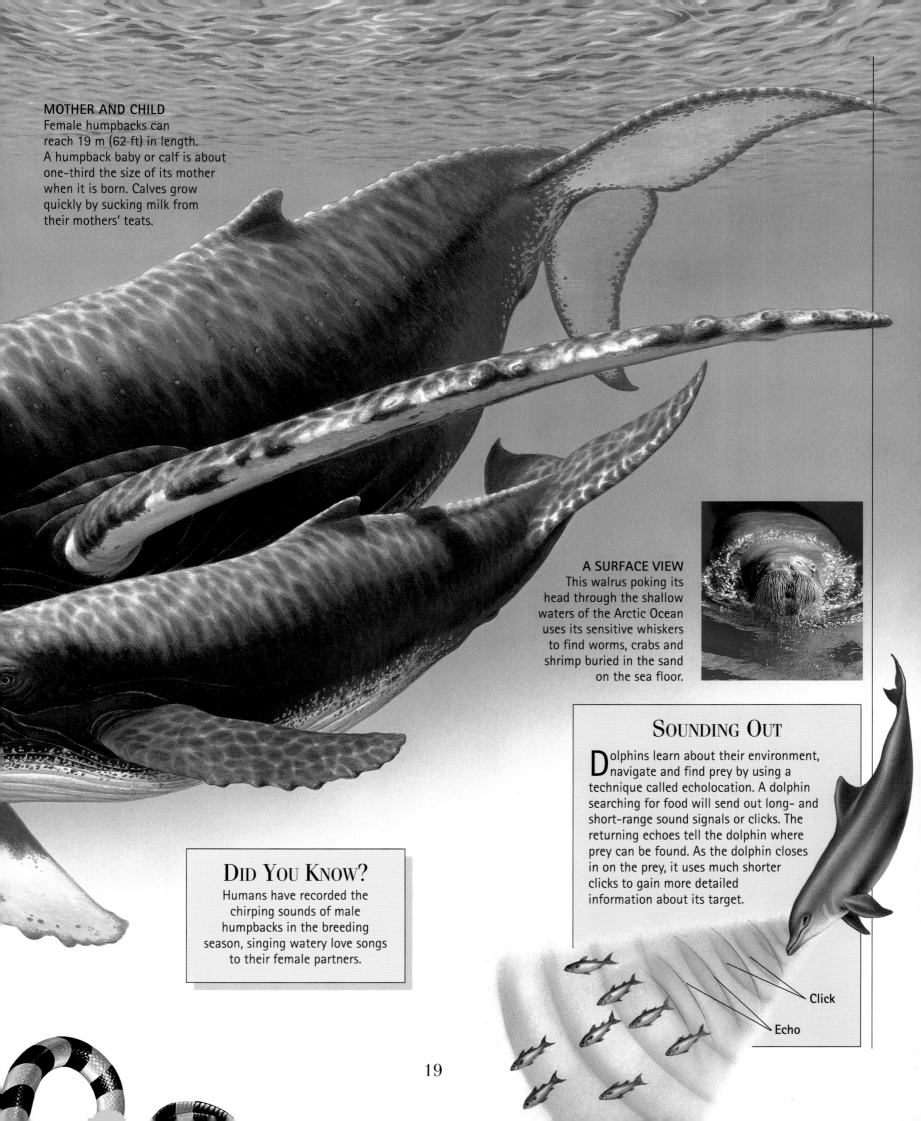

MOTHER AND CHILD
Female humpbacks can reach 19 m (62 ft) in length. A humpback baby or calf is about one-third the size of its mother when it is born. Calves grow quickly by sucking milk from their mothers' teats.

A SURFACE VIEW
This walrus poking its head through the shallow waters of the Arctic Ocean uses its sensitive whiskers to find worms, crabs and shrimp buried in the sand on the sea floor.

SOUNDING OUT

Dolphins learn about their environment, navigate and find prey by using a technique called echolocation. A dolphin searching for food will send out long- and short-range sound signals or clicks. The returning echoes tell the dolphin where prey can be found. As the dolphin closes in on the prey, it uses much shorter clicks to gain more detailed information about its target.

DID YOU KNOW?

Humans have recorded the chirping sounds of male humpbacks in the breeding season, singing watery love songs to their female partners.

Click

Echo

Coral Reefs

Brightly colored fish and thousands of other sea creatures live in the shelter of coral reefs. These marine homes grow in warm shallow seas and are built by coral animals, or polyps, with soft bodies and mouths that are ringed by stinging tentacles. The polyps construct thimble-shaped skeletons of limestone around themselves. As the polyps grow upwards, they keep dividing in two. They leave their skeletons behind them, however, and these fuse together to make a coral reef. A living mass of growing polyps always forms a film of flesh on top of the skeletons. Each polyp has many round plant cells living in its body and these cells make food from a combination of sunlight, water and carbon dioxide (a process called photosynthesis). The corals are able to catch their own food with their stinging tentacles, but most of the food they eat is made by the plant cells. Coral reefs need the food from these plant cells to grow quickly.

HIDING OUT
A clownfish lives and hides from its enemies within the tentacles of the coral reef anemone. It escapes being stung by covering itself in a layer of mucus from the anemone. The coral is fooled into thinking that the fish is part of itself.

CORAL WATCHING
Coral reefs, such as this one at Taveuni Island in the Pacific Ocean, attract snorkelers and divers from all over the world. But coral reefs are very fragile, and some are being damaged by human contact.

CORAL COMMUNITIES
Many species of coral, such as sea fan coral, hard brain coral, bubble coral and soft fire coral, grow together. They live side by side with goldfish, giant clams, surgeonfish and many other sea dwellers.

CORAL SPAWNING
When coral spawn, some release their eggs and sperm to be fertilized in the water; others release sperm to fertilize the egg inside the polyp.

CORAL POLYPS
These tiny coral animals form coral colonies of different shapes and colors. Plant cells live within the tissues of most corals and these help the coral polyp to produce its limestone skeleton.

Tentacles

Mouth

CROWDED HOUSE
Crustaceans, fish, sea urchins, mollusks and clams are some of the many creatures that live on a coral reef.

Butterfly fish

LEAFY SEA DRAGON
The leafy sea dragon is a type of seahorse. Its leaf-like flaps of skin help it to blend with the kelp fronds.

Camouflage

The world under the sea can be a dangerous place to live. Sea creatures often use camouflage to hide from their natural enemies. Some fish change color to match their surroundings, some take on extraordinary shapes to look like sea plants, some are almost completely transparent and are very difficult to see, while others bury themselves in the sand. Crabs are experts at disguise. Many attach algae to their bodies; others add sponges or sea squirts. The butterfly fish, shown on the left, is very clever at camouflage. Its real eyes are small and have stripes through them. But it also seems to have a large eye near its tail. These two sets of "eyes" confuse the butterfly fish's enemies. Which is the front and which is the back? An enemy does not know which way the fish will flee if attacked.

STILL AS STONE
This purple stonefish matches the coral-covered rocks on the sea floor. It has sharp spines that can inject deadly poison.

LURKING IN THE SHADOWS
Blending perfectly with the backdrop of sponges and corals, the scorpion fish waits for prey, such as fish and crustaceans, to swim close to its jaws.

EYE SPY
Some creatures bury themselves under the sand to hide from enemies. Only their large, rock-like eyeballs remain exposed.

SEE-THROUGH SHRIMP

Can you see the shrimp in this picture? It is completely transparent, except for a few glowing markings. It lives on colorful anemones.

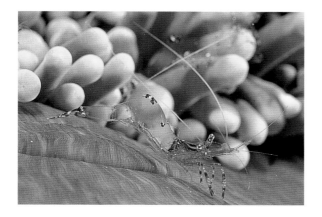

COVERED WITH COLOR

Many sea creatures use color as a camouflage. An octopus has small, elastic bags of color in its skin. When the bags are stretched, they become dark. When the bags shrink, they are almost white. Different bags can be stretched or compressed in different parts of the body. This means an octopus can change color to match surrounding rocks.

RED ALERT
A red-and-white hawkfish camouflages itself by darting in and out of red-branched coral.

SUCKED IN
The pipefish has adapted its shape and color to match the kelp and coral that grow under the sea. It sucks in tiny animals through its small mouth.

MOBILE HOME
The hermit crab makes its home in a mollusk shell. As it grows, the crab moves out of its old home and finds a more spacious one.

ANTARCTICA
This huge, ice-covered continent around the South Pole is the coldest place on Earth. Only during the summer does the temperature ever rise above the freezing point. The ocean around Antarctica, however, teems with plants and animals—food for many seals, birds and whales.

STRANGE BUT TRUE
The aptly named ice fish lives in polar seas. While the blood of most fish freezes at about -35°C (-32°F), the ice fish has special chemicals in its blood to stop it from freezing.

AN EASY WINNER
The Weddell seal holds the seal record for deep-sea diving. It can dive to about 1,970 ft (600 m) and stay under the water for more than an hour.

EMPEROR PENGUINS
These are the largest and most colorful of all the penguins. They usually walk upright, but they can also toboggan over the snow, using their feet and flippers to skim along the icy surface on their chests.

· LIFE IN THE SEA ·

Polar Seas

The icy seas of the polar regions are the wildest and coldest seas on Earth. The Arctic Ocean around the North Pole is covered by permanent ice and floating pack ice. It has many unique animals, such as polar bears, bearded and hooded seals and musk oxen. The Southern Ocean around the South Pole encircles the huge continent of Antarctica, which is buried beneath ice. Seals such as the crabeater, elephant and leopard seals inhabit these southern waters with 16 different kinds of penguin. Winter at the poles is long, dark and freezing. Some polar animals migrate, but most have adapted to these bitter conditions by growing special feathers or thick fur. Others have layers of fat to protect them from the cold. In summer it is light all the time, and the polar seas teem with life. Rich sea currents sweep up nutrients from the ocean depths to help the plant plankton grow. This is eaten by tiny krill, the main food for many polar creatures.

TIP OF THE ICEBERG
The Southern Ocean is filled with floating icebergs, which have broken off from the ice shelf. About 90 per cent of an iceberg is underwater, so the huge area we see above water is only the top of its immense structure.

PUFFIN
A tasty catch
dangles from a
puffin's curious bill.

ATTACK!
A hungry polar bear breaks through
the ice with its paws, snaring a baby
beluga swimming below. The bear's sharp
claws and teeth are like fishing hooks.
Scientists have learned recently that polar bears
bite or scratch a whale's blowhole so that it cannot
breathe. This makes it easier for polar bears to pull
these small whales onto the ice to eat them.

A POLE APART
In the summer, temperatures
in the Arctic rise to well
above freezing,
especially in the
coastal areas of
the bordering
continents.
Caribou
move north
to feed, and
wild flowers
bloom across
the land.

Europe

The Arctic

Canada

Greenland

IN QUICK PURSUIT
Killer whales are fast swimmers. They have cone-shaped teeth to catch and chew fish and smaller mammals.

Ocean Meadows

The ocean is like a giant meadow, providing food for all its creatures. The food web that operates under water is a complex system where large creatures prey on smaller creatures. Killer whales eat seals and sealions, which feed on fish and squid. Salmon enjoy small fish, which eat plankton— the tiny plants (phytoplankton) and animals (zooplankton) that float in the sunlight of the surface waters. Plankton is the basic source of food for ocean animals, and plants are the most important link in the food web. They use water, carbon dioxide and energy from sunlight to make plant food. If links in the food web are ever lost, others will take their place. Sardines once played a vital role in the food web off the coast of California. But they became scarce when too many of them were fished, and anchovies took their place.

PHYTOPLANKTON
The sunlit, upper layer of the ocean teems with microscopic life, such as plant plankton, the basic food of the sea.

Uncoiled tube

Coiled tube

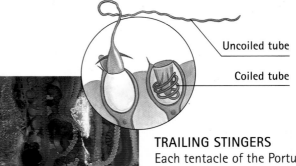

ZOOPLANKTON
Many kinds of microscopic animal plankton swim in the ocean. Some are the larvae of fish, which have just hatched, while others are small crustaceans, such as shrimp.

TRAILING STINGERS
Each tentacle of the Portuguese man o' war has many stinging cells and a sac containing a coiled, barbed tube. When a fish touches the cell, the tube uncoils, pierces the skin and delivers the venomous poison.

SEALIONS AND SEALS
These are the natural prey of large meat-eating mammals and fish, such as whales and sharks.

PREYING ON SMALL FISH
With mouth open and sharp teeth ready, a salmon swims after a school of herring.

THE WORLD OF PLANKTON
This satellite image of the world's oceans shows where plant plankton are common. Some areas have more plankton than others and the colors on the map indicate these from the most (red), through yellow, green and blue, to the least (violet). The grey parts show where there are gaps in the information collected.

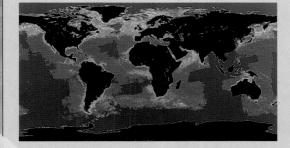

TINY LINKS
Krill are small, shrimplike creatures, which live in vast numbers in the Southern Ocean. Whales, seals and seabirds all feed on krill, and they are an important link in the food web in this part of the world.

GIANT RAY
Not all large animals in the food web eat large prey. The manta ray glides through the water, mouth agape, sieving out tiny fish and crustaceans.

TORPEDO POWER
A squid speeds through the water, its torpedo-shaped body shooting out a water jet behind it, and grabs a fish with the special suckers on the ends of its tentacles. As it is a very fast swimmer, a squid can catch prey easily.

FILTERING THROUGH
Herring feed on plankton, which they filter from the water.

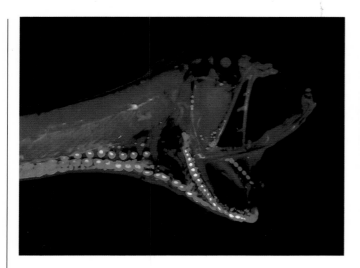

SLOANE'S VIPER
This viperfish has light organs, or photophores on its belly. Despite being only about 1 ft (30 cm) long, it has impressive jaws and teeth. It is one of the most feared of the deep-sea predators.

SWALLOWER
This fish has a hugely expandable stomach and is known as a swallower. It is able to eat fish that are longer and larger than itself.

Life in the Twilight Zone

Imagine the world at dusk. It is hard to see in the gloom, and shapes blur into the blackness. This is the atmosphere of the twilight zone, 656–3,280 ft (200–1,000 m) below the sunlit surface of the sea. Only blue light remains in this cold, deep-sea zone, the home of many interesting creatures that have adapted to life in this part of the ocean. Regalecus, the king of the herring, shares this murky world with lampris, a silver-spotted fish. Giant squid, which sometimes rise to the surface at night, loom in the depths with swordfish and big-eye tuna. Many of the fish in the twilight zone glow in the dark. They have bacteria that produces light—a process called bioluminescence. These animals use bioluminescence in different ways: some send out light patterns to attract mates in the darkness; several kinds of fish have bioluminescent organs on the lower half of their bodies, which they use for camouflage; others temporarily blind their predators with sudden flashes of light.

DID YOU KNOW?
Some kinds of fish and shrimp use bioluminescence to camouflage themselves. They have light organs on the lower half of their bodies that they use to blend in with light filtering from the surface. When predators look upwards, they cannot see the shape of their prey.

MOLA MOLA
This ocean sunfish has a very distinctive body shape and can be up to 10 ft (3 m) long.

KING-OF-THE-SALMON
Native Americans call the ribbonfish king-of-the-salmon. They believe it leads Pacific salmon back to the rivers to spawn when the breeding season begins.

ANGLERFISH

The female anglerfish has a luminous lure. The bulblike bait on her head contains luminescent bacteria. This attracts prey to the anglerfish, which saves energy by not having to hunt for food.

LANTERNFISH

There are huge numbers of these fish in the deep sea. They are called lanternfish because they have light organs on their heads and bodies.

COLONIAL SEA SQUIRT

The sacklike body of the sea squirt has openings through which water enters and leaves.

FLASHLIGHT FISH

This fish can be seen from a distance of 98 ft (30 m) in the dark depths of the ocean.

SQUID

Many squid live in the ocean depths. They have well-developed senses and can propel themselves quickly through the water.

VIPERFISH

The curving fangs of the small viperfish make it a dangerous predator.

SEEING IN THE DARK

Flashlight fish are found in caves at the bottom of coral reefs. They have large light organs under their eyes that contain luminous, or glowing, bacteria. The fish use these light organs to feed, and to communicate with other flashlight fish. But glowing in the dark can create problems when trying to avoid predators. The flashlight fish is able to cover the light organ with a screen of pigmented tissue, called a melanphore. This means it can turn the light on and off— just like a flashlight.

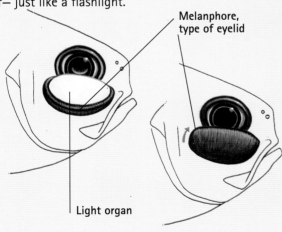

Melanphore, type of eyelid

Light organ

HATCHETFISH

These fish have light organs underneath their bodies that confuse predators swimming beneath them. Their eyes have large lenses that help them see small, glowing fish and shellfish.

SCALY DRAGONFISH

The thick, jellylike layer that covers the scales of this fish contains light organs.

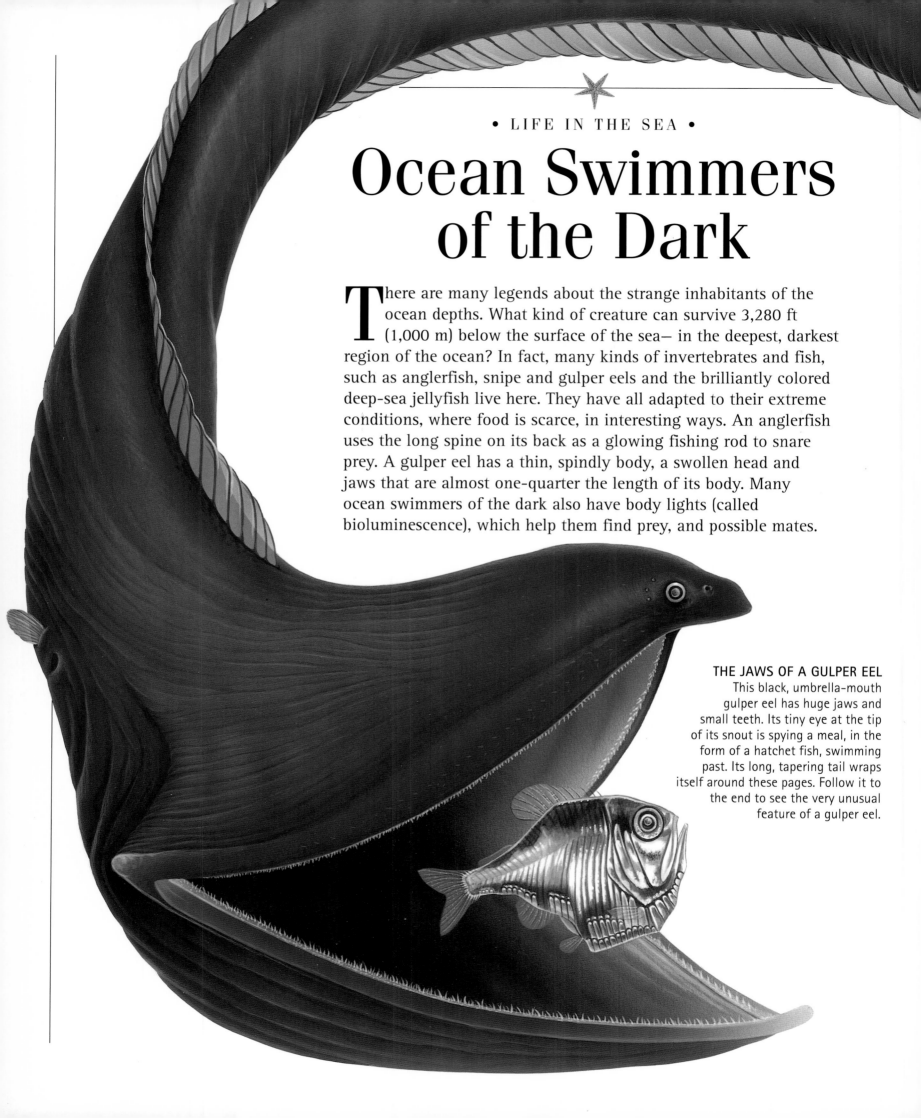

Ocean Swimmers of the Dark

There are many legends about the strange inhabitants of the ocean depths. What kind of creature can survive 3,280 ft (1,000 m) below the surface of the sea— in the deepest, darkest region of the ocean? In fact, many kinds of invertebrates and fish, such as anglerfish, snipe and gulper eels and the brilliantly colored deep-sea jellyfish live here. They have all adapted to their extreme conditions, where food is scarce, in interesting ways. An anglerfish uses the long spine on its back as a glowing fishing rod to snare prey. A gulper eel has a thin, spindly body, a swollen head and jaws that are almost one-quarter the length of its body. Many ocean swimmers of the dark also have body lights (called bioluminescence), which help them find prey, and possible mates.

THE JAWS OF A GULPER EEL
This black, umbrella-mouth gulper eel has huge jaws and small teeth. Its tiny eye at the tip of its snout is spying a meal, in the form of a hatchet fish, swimming past. Its long, tapering tail wraps itself around these pages. Follow it to the end to see the very unusual feature of a gulper eel.

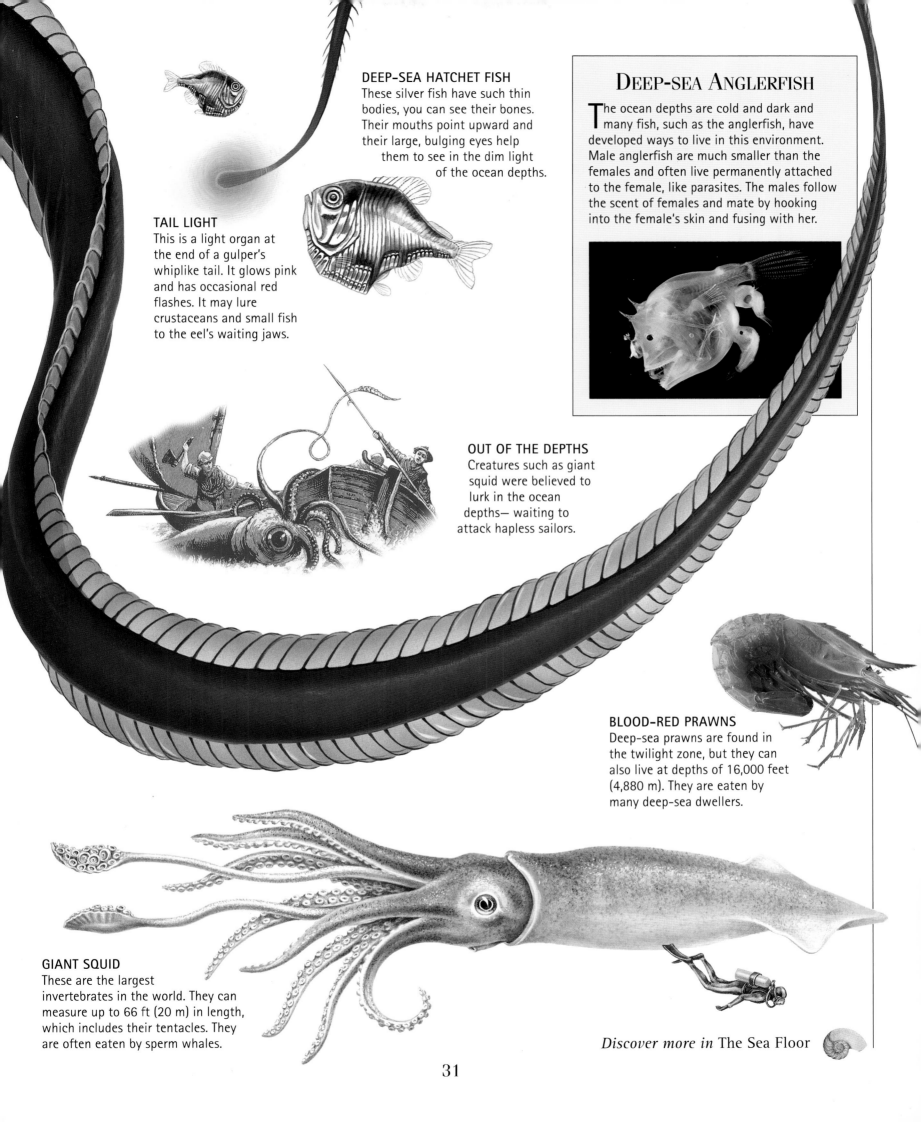

DEEP-SEA HATCHET FISH
These silver fish have such thin bodies, you can see their bones. Their mouths point upward and their large, bulging eyes help them to see in the dim light of the ocean depths.

TAIL LIGHT
This is a light organ at the end of a gulper's whiplike tail. It glows pink and has occasional red flashes. It may lure crustaceans and small fish to the eel's waiting jaws.

DEEP-SEA ANGLERFISH
The ocean depths are cold and dark and many fish, such as the anglerfish, have developed ways to live in this environment. Male anglerfish are much smaller than the females and often live permanently attached to the female, like parasites. The males follow the scent of females and mate by hooking into the female's skin and fusing with her.

OUT OF THE DEPTHS
Creatures such as giant squid were believed to lurk in the ocean depths— waiting to attack hapless sailors.

BLOOD-RED PRAWNS
Deep-sea prawns are found in the twilight zone, but they can also live at depths of 16,000 feet (4,880 m). They are eaten by many deep-sea dwellers.

GIANT SQUID
These are the largest invertebrates in the world. They can measure up to 66 ft (20 m) in length, which includes their tentacles. They are often eaten by sperm whales.

Discover more in The Sea Floor

31

Life on the Ocean Floor

The ocean floor is cold, dark and still. The temperature never rises to more than just above freezing, and there is no light. This means there is little food, for plants cannot grow without energy from the sun. Deep-sea dwellers filter, sieve and sift the water and mud on the ocean floor to find tiny pieces of food that have dropped from the surface of the sea. These creatures of the deep have adapted well to their demanding environment. Some have soft, squishy bodies and large heads. They do not need strong skins and bones because there are no waves in this part of the ocean. Many are blind and move slowly through the water. Gigantic sea spiders, gutless worms and glass rope sponges are some of the unusual creatures that live in the inky blackness of the ocean floor.

Seeing in the dark
The US Navy submersible *Alvin* can carry its two crew members to a depth of 13,000 feet (3,960 m).

Eelpout
These long fish live near underwater vents and eat tube worms.

Muscling in
Mussels and giant clams live on bacteria inside their bodies.

TRIPOD FISH

The tripod fish is one of the most bizarre of the deep-sea creatures. It has three very long fins that it uses to hold itself above the ocean floor. From this position, it watches and waits patiently for unsuspecting prey. Scientists believe the tripod fish adopts the pose of a stilt-walker because it is easier to smell food in the currents above the ocean floor.

Black smokers
These mineral chimneys can be up to 33 ft (10 m) high, and occur mainly near ocean ridges. Deep-sea creatures gather around the chimneys, which blast black smoke and hot water rich in sulphur from vents at the top. These animals make their own food using the sulphur and bacteria.

Tube worms
Tube worms are found in clusters. One end of the white tube is attached to the ocean floor; a red plume, or breathing organ, emerges from the other end.

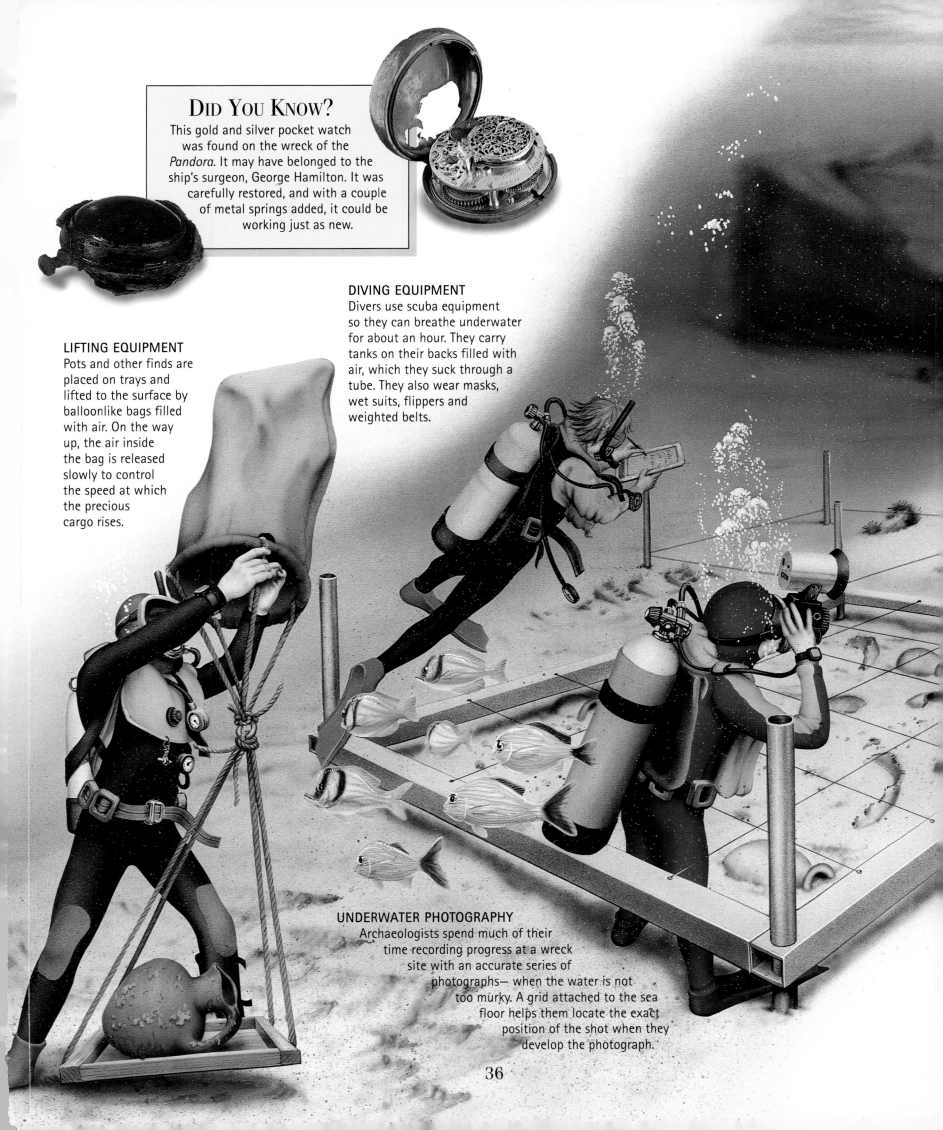

DID YOU KNOW?

This gold and silver pocket watch was found on the wreck of the *Pandora*. It may have belonged to the ship's surgeon, George Hamilton. It was carefully restored, and with a couple of metal springs added, it could be working just as new.

DIVING EQUIPMENT

Divers use scuba equipment so they can breathe underwater for about an hour. They carry tanks on their backs filled with air, which they suck through a tube. They also wear masks, wet suits, flippers and weighted belts.

LIFTING EQUIPMENT

Pots and other finds are placed on trays and lifted to the surface by balloonlike bags filled with air. On the way up, the air inside the bag is released slowly to control the speed at which the precious cargo rises.

UNDERWATER PHOTOGRAPHY

Archaeologists spend much of their time recording progress at a wreck site with an accurate series of photographs— when the water is not too murky. A grid attached to the sea floor helps them locate the exact position of the shot when they develop the photograph.

Wrecks and Treasures

Many wrecks lie on the ocean floor— silent reminders of times past. Raging storms, little knowledge of navigation, poorly charted seas, fierce sea battles and bad luck were responsible for most of the shipwrecks. These wrecks now provide shelter for fish and other creatures of the sea. Scuba divers visit those in shallow waters, eager to find out if there is anything of value on the wreck. The pottery, coins, bottles and other material divers discover are valuable clues. They show how their owners once lived. One of the most fascinating shipwrecks is the sunken luxury liner the *Titanic*. It lies more than 2 $1/2$ miles (4 km) beneath the sea and can only be reached by a small submarine called a submersible. People said that the *Titanic* was unsinkable. But on its first voyage in 1912, it rammed into an iceberg and sank quickly with few survivors. As the swirling black waters engulfed the sinking ship, the orchestra continued to play on the deck.

RECOVERING ARTIFACTS
A diver gently examines an encrusted Roman storage jar, lodged on the bottom of the Mediterranean Sea. Octopuses often crawl into empty jars they find on the ocean floor.

BLUNDERBUSS
This short musket and its lead balls of ammunition were recovered from the *Pandora*. It sank off the coast of northern Australia in 1791.

• EXPLORING THE OCEANS •

Early Exploration

In 1872, HMS *Challenger* left England on a four-year journey to explore the world's oceans. The scientists on board wanted to study the sea in a way that had never been done before. They hoped to find the answers to questions such as "How deep is the ocean?" and "Are all seas equally salty?" They intended to collect data and provide research for the development of oceanography, thestudy of the oceans. These keen ocean explorers dredged the sea floor, and took rock and mud samples from the Atlantic, the Pacific and the Indian oceans. They discovered thousands of new plants and bizarre sea creatures; they recorded the temperatures of deep seas and charted the movements of the main ocean currents. The scientists carefully recorded all the details they observed during their expedition, and their findings filled a staggering 50 volumes. They realized there was still a huge amount to learn about the sea, but the study of the oceans had definitely begun.

INSIDE THE CHALLENGER
The *Challenger* was fitted with special laboratories so scientists on board could examine carefully the different plants and animals they dredged from the sea floor.

SEA THERMOMETER
The scientists on the *Challenger* used sea thermometers to record and chart the highest and lowest water temperatures in the oceans.

THE JOURNEY
The *Challenger* sailed past Cape Challenger, the southernmost point of remote Kerguelen Island in the southern Indian Ocean, on the first leg of its journey. It traveled via the Pacific Ocean and the Strait of Magellan before returning to England.

SAILING THE OCEAN BLUE

The *Challenger* expedition was headed by Professor Wyville Thomson. His assistant was John Murray, a young geologist. Captain Nares and his crew sailed the vessel through many treacherous seas.

ON THE OCEAN FLOOR

Deep-sea dredges such as this were used on board the *Challenger* to scoop up plants and animals from the ocean floor. They were weighted and lowered into the sea. Towropes attached to the ship dragged them to the bottom of the ocean.

Dredge   Weight

A WORLD AWAY

Members of the *Challenger's* expedition recorded the animals and environments they saw on their voyage.

DRAWN IN

These drawings that were made during the *Challenger's* trip show the bodies of jellyfish, starfish and brittlestars.

...rates little by
...e masts and
...ring the next
...llapses. After
...collapse and
...ter 80 years,
...ly filled with
...ship is stable.

1 year

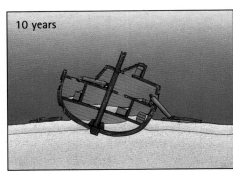

10 years

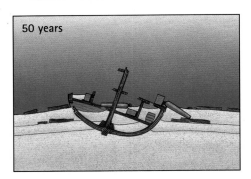

50 years

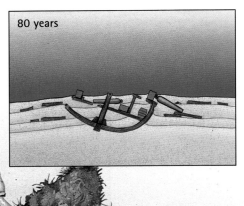

80 years

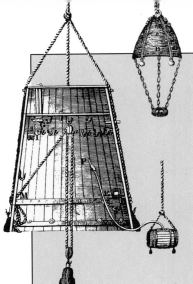

THE HISTORY OF DIVING

For more than 2,000 years, humans have explored the world beneath the waves. The ancient Greeks dove for treasure and valuable sea sponges. The diving bell was invented in 1721 to help divers remain under water for longer periods of time. Divers in the mid-1800s wore heavy canvas diving suits with copper helmets. In the 1940s, Jacques Cousteau and Emile Gagnan invented a self-contained underwater breathing apparatus (SCUBA). Deep-sea divers in the 1970s wore diving suits that looked just like astronauts' spacesuits.

ADVENTUROUS DIVING
Dr Edmund Halley built the first diving bell and inspired others to design many other types of diving bells (as shown on the left). They allowed divers to explore the world beneath the ocean while breathing the air trapped inside the bells.

HARD-HAT DIVING
This early 1900s diving suit had a large metal helmet with a valve designed to keep fresh air flowing through the helmet. Air was pumped down a pipe from a boat on the surface.

FIRST AIR TANK
This 1950s aqualung, or breathing apparatus, is similar to the one designed by Jacques Cousteau and Emile Gagnan. It is strapped to the back, and the mouthpiece is attached to air cylinders.

Discover more in Submersibles

DISI
A wrecked ship disinteg
little through the years. 1
rigging break up first. Du
10 years, the upper deck cc
50 years, the outer timbers
sediment builds up. A
the hull has complete
sediment, and the

CLEARING AWAY THE SEDIMENT
Marine archaeologists use giant
vacuum cleaners called air-lifting
pipes to suck up sediment from
the ocean floor.

EXCAVATION GRID
A series of movable aluminium grid
frames that are locked together help marine
archaeologists cover a shipwreck site in a
systematic way. Starting in the first square on their
giant underwater chessboard, divers move from one
marked square to the next, recording what they find
in each, until they have covered the whole area.

Submersibles

The ocean floor is many miles below the surface. While the safe maximum depth for scuba diving is 165 ft (50 m), the deepest parts of the ocean may be 7 miles (11 km) below the surface. The only way to reach such depths is by a submersible, a small submarine that dives from its "mother" ship. The United States submersible *Alvin* and the French vessel *Nautile* have visited the underwater site of the sunken ocean liner the *Titanic*. The crew of *Alvin* used an even smaller robot submersible, *Jason Jr.,* to probe inside places too small or too dangerous for *Alvin* to go itself. Larger submersible structures have also been used for research. The Hydrolab was launched in Florida in 1968, and for 18 years was the underwater home of scientists who observed and recorded the habits and behavior of lobsters, snapper, grouper and the hundreds of creatures living on a coral reef.

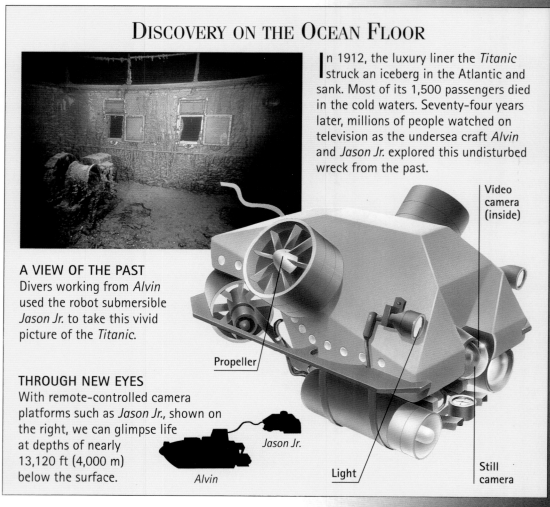

DISCOVERY ON THE OCEAN FLOOR

In 1912, the luxury liner the *Titanic* struck an iceberg in the Atlantic and sank. Most of its 1,500 passengers died in the cold waters. Seventy-four years later, millions of people watched on television as the undersea craft *Alvin* and *Jason Jr.* explored this undisturbed wreck from the past.

A VIEW OF THE PAST
Divers working from *Alvin* used the robot submersible *Jason Jr.* to take this vivid picture of the *Titanic*.

THROUGH NEW EYES
With remote-controlled camera platforms such as *Jason Jr.,* shown on the right, we can glimpse life at depths of nearly 13,120 ft (4,000 m) below the surface.

Jason Jr.

Alvin

Propeller

Video camera (inside)

Light

Still camera

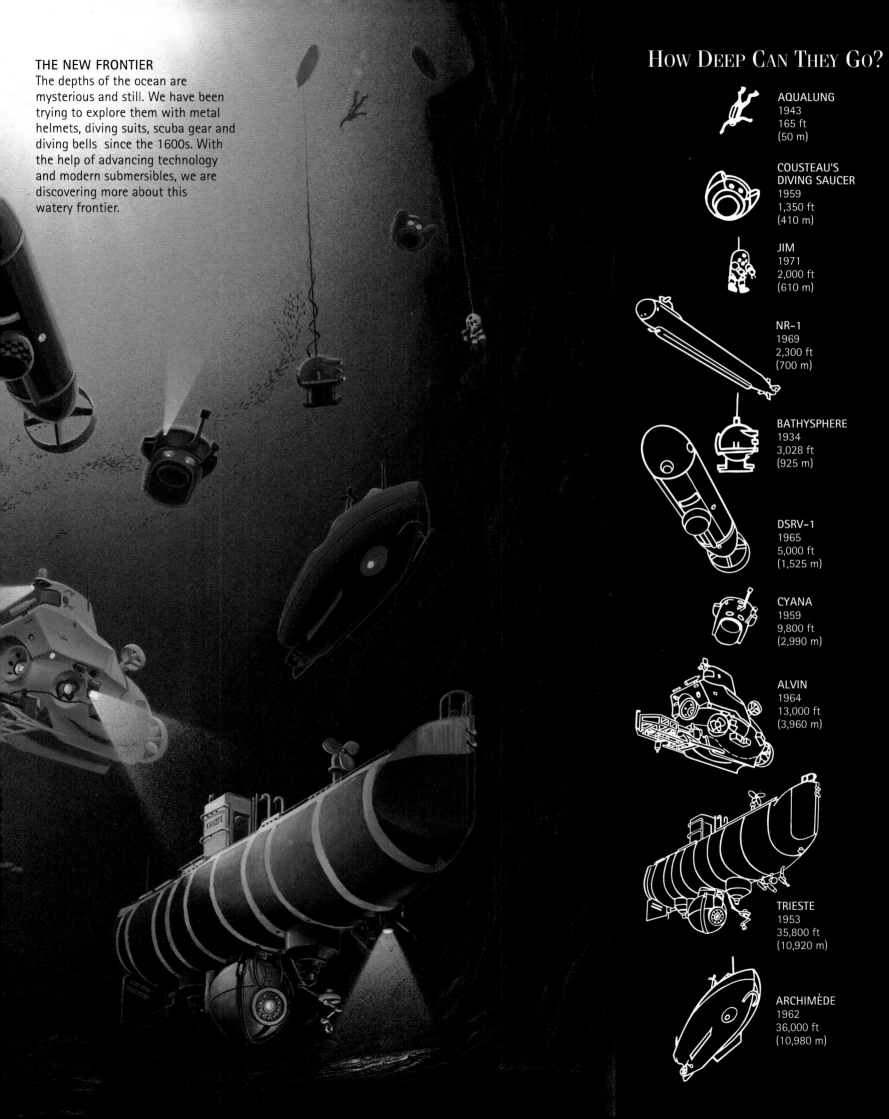

THE NEW FRONTIER

The depths of the ocean are mysterious and still. We have been trying to explore them with metal helmets, diving suits, scuba gear and diving bells since the 1600s. With the help of advancing technology and modern submersibles, we are discovering more about this watery frontier.

HOW DEEP CAN THEY GO?

AQUALUNG
1943
165 ft
(50 m)

COUSTEAU'S DIVING SAUCER
1959
1,350 ft
(410 m)

JIM
1971
2,000 ft
(610 m)

NR-1
1969
2,300 ft
(700 m)

BATHYSPHERE
1934
3,028 ft
(925 m)

DSRV-1
1965
5,000 ft
(1,525 m)

CYANA
1959
9,800 ft
(2,990 m)

ALVIN
1964
13,000 ft
(3,960 m)

TRIESTE
1953
35,800 ft
(10,920 m)

ARCHIMÈDE
1962
36,000 ft
(10,980 m)

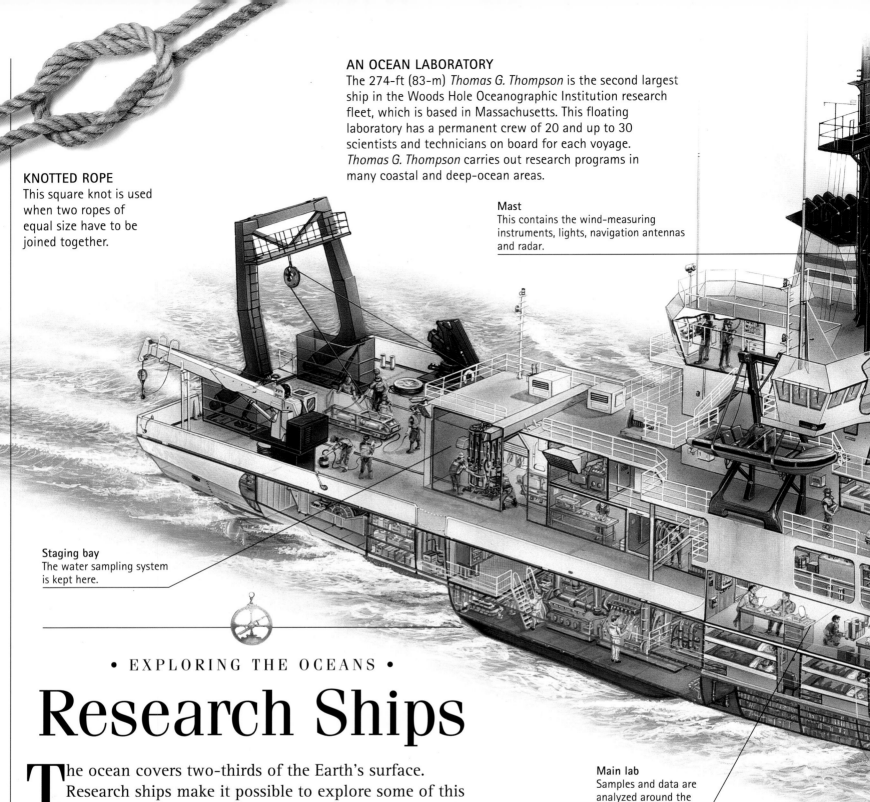

KNOTTED ROPE
This square knot is used when two ropes of equal size have to be joined together.

AN OCEAN LABORATORY
The 274-ft (83-m) *Thomas G. Thompson* is the second largest ship in the Woods Hole Oceanographic Institution research fleet, which is based in Massachusetts. This floating laboratory has a permanent crew of 20 and up to 30 scientists and technicians on board for each voyage. *Thomas G. Thompson* carries out research programs in many coastal and deep-ocean areas.

Mast
This contains the wind-measuring instruments, lights, navigation antennas and radar.

Staging bay
The water sampling system is kept here.

• EXPLORING THE OCEANS •

Research Ships

The ocean covers two-thirds of the Earth's surface. Research ships make it possible to explore some of this enormous area. They are specially equipped so that scientists can study deep currents and the structure of the ocean floor; learn how the ocean interacts with the Earth's atmosphere and how this affects climate and weather; and how natural and human disturbances, such as burning fossil fuels and releasing carbon dioxide into the air, affect the oceans. These vessels carry sophisticated navigation and communications systems, cranes and winches for their sampling and measuring devices, special mooring cables and tanks for live specimens. The requirements of their on-board laboratories often change from voyage to voyage. The ships stay in touch with their home ports by satellite.

Main lab
Samples and data are analyzed around the clock in the main lab.

WATER SAMPLERS
These scientists are preparing to send water sample bottles to the bottom of the ocean. Valuable information can be obtained by analyzing these samples.

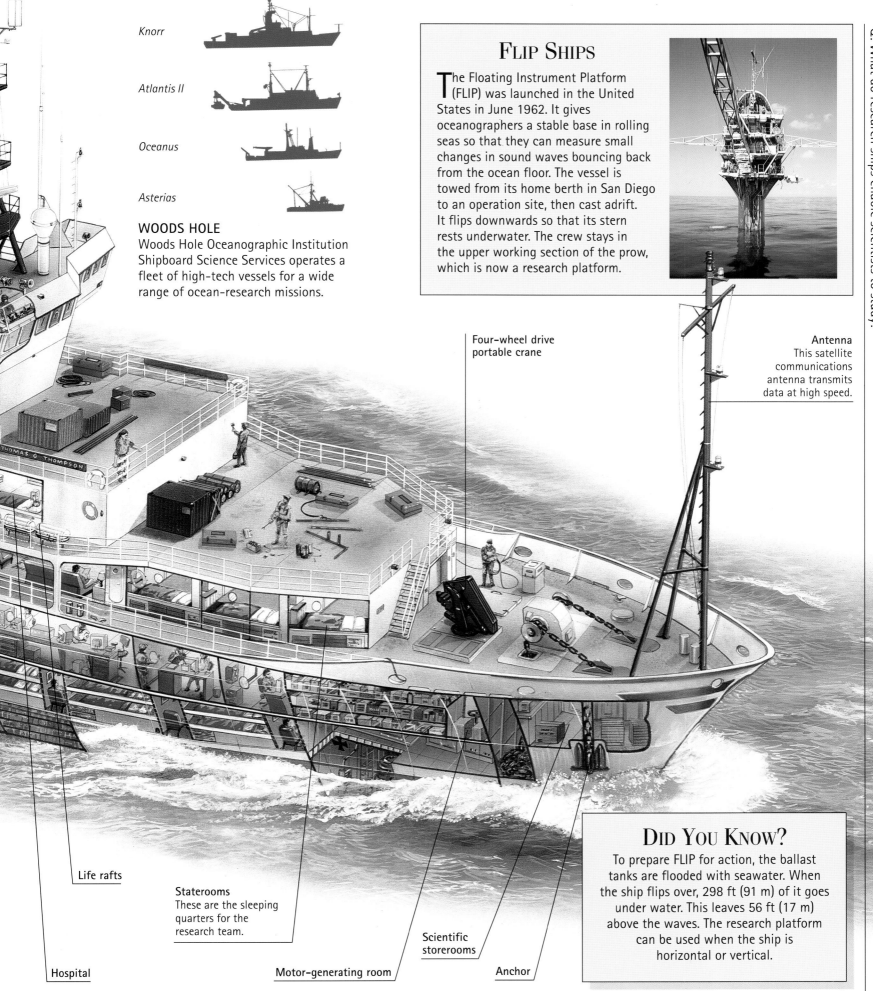

Knorr

Atlantis II

Oceanus

Asterias

WOODS HOLE

Woods Hole Oceanographic Institution Shipboard Science Services operates a fleet of high-tech vessels for a wide range of ocean-research missions.

FLIP SHIPS

The Floating Instrument Platform (FLIP) was launched in the United States in June 1962. It gives oceanographers a stable base in rolling seas so that they can measure small changes in sound waves bouncing back from the ocean floor. The vessel is towed from its home berth in San Diego to an operation site, then cast adrift. It flips downwards so that its stern rests underwater. The crew stays in the upper working section of the prow, which is now a research platform.

Four-wheel drive portable crane

Antenna
This satellite communications antenna transmits data at high speed.

Life rafts

Staterooms
These are the sleeping quarters for the research team.

Hospital

Motor-generating room

Scientific storerooms

Anchor

DID YOU KNOW?

To prepare FLIP for action, the ballast tanks are flooded with seawater. When the ship flips over, 298 ft (91 m) of it goes under water. This leaves 56 ft (17 m) above the waves. The research platform can be used when the ship is horizontal or vertical.

Discover more in Wrecks and Treasures

Sea Legends

Early seafarers and explorers, searching for new lands, faced daily perils in unknown seas. They braved storms, icebergs, fog, hidden reefs and the unsettling calm, waiting for a flurry of wind to catch the sails. Sailors told of huge sea monsters; of mermaids and mermen; and of Neptune, the fiery god of the sea. Rumors and exaggerated tales of true and imagined sea creatures were exchanged at every port. Cartographers, drawing detailed maps of new routes and countries, even included pictures of dragon-like monsters roaring their way around the world's oceans. Many nations have legends about the sea. The ancient Greeks told stories of sirens (part woman, part bird) whose sweet songs lured mariners to their death on jagged rocks. Ulysses, one of the heroes of Greek mythology, had to put wax in his sailors' ears to stop them from jumping into the sea as they sailed past the sirens' island. He lashed himself to the mast so that he could hear their singing, but not be charmed by it.

SEA MONSTERS

Do they really exist? Or are they exaggerated versions of real sea giants, such as sawfish, narwhals or humpback whales? The octopus-like sea monster wrapping itself around this ship is said to be a kraken, a mythical creature that appears off the shores of Norway. It must seem very real to the sailors clinging desperately to the ropes on this sinking ship.

WOMEN OF THE WAVES

Mermaids often appear in legends, with long flowing tresses of hair, decorated with delicate shell combs. Stories tell of mermaids enticing humans into the sea, and drowning them in its depths.

THE LOCH NESS MONSTER

The sea is not the only water surrounded by mysteries and myths. The deep lake called Loch Ness in northern Scotland is a strange and lonely place, often shrouded by mist. Visitors claim to have seen and photographed a monster rising silently above the surface, and disappearing mysteriously. Scientists have investigated the sightings but have never found the monster. Nor have they proved that it does not exist. If you visit the lake, you can see a video of the elusive creature "Nessie."

SEA GOD

The Romans believed that Neptune was the god of the sea. He ruled the many creatures that lived below the waves.

MONSTER ACT

This photograph is said to prove once and for all that the Loch Ness Monster really exists. But is this dark shape really a monster? Could it be a whale or a mystery submarine?

SHOWTIME FOR NESSIE!

45

GHOSTLY WATCH
On the lonely night watch, these sailors are chilled by the sight of a fully rigged phantom ship sailing silently past in the mist.

Where Did They Go?

There are many ocean mysteries that have fascinated and frustrated people for hundreds of years. One region in the world that seems particularly mysterious is the Bermuda Triangle, which lies between Bermuda, Florida and Puerto Rico. Many ships and aircraft have vanished completely in the Triangle. No one has been able to explain their disappearance, and their wrecks have never been found. Strong storms, powerful currents and deep seas probably claimed any wreckage quickly. But what of the *Mary Celeste* and its missing crew? In 1872, this American ship was found floating, in seaworthy condition, in the middle of the Atlantic Ocean. There were no sailors in sight, and few clues as to where they had gone. One of the most intriguing mysteries from the past surrounds the legendary continent of Atlantis. Plato, a Greek philosopher, wrote that it sank into the Atlantic Ocean. But did it ever really exist? Many people believe the story of Atlantis was based on the Greek island of Thera, which was ruptured by volcanic explosions.

SAILING SOLO
When the *Mary Celeste* was discovered abandoned and drifting, the lifeboat and navigational instruments were missing. Did the captain order the crew to leave the ship, and with his wife and two-year-old daughter, take to the lifeboat and the endless horizon of sea?

STRANGE BUT TRUE
Did the *Mary Celeste* sail itself? The last log entry put the ship near the Azores, some 700 miles (1,130 km) and 9 days away from where it was found.

FLIGHT 19'S LAST MISSION

On 5 December 1945, the sky droned with the engine noises of five torpedo bombers on a training flight from Florida. But flying across the Bermuda Triangle, the whole squadron vanished. During the last radio contact with their base, they said they were low on fuel and might have to land in the water. Rescue crews scoured the ocean for five days. They discovered no trace of the missing men or planes.

THE LOST KINGDOM

The Greek philosopher Plato was the first to write about the lost civilization of Atlantis. He said that thousands of years ago there was a large island in the Atlantic Ocean. The temples were decorated with gold, silver, copper and ivory; the people were very wealthy and lived in magnificent buildings. But, according to Plato, the people became greedy and dishonest, and the gods decided to punish them. During one day and night, violent eruptions shook the island and it disappeared, forever, into the sea.

Plato

MAPPED OUT

A map from the seventeenth century shows Atlantis as a very large island, midway between America and the Pillars of Hercules, at the entrance to the Mediterranean Sea.

Mysteries of Migration

Many of the animals in the world make long journeys, or migrations, each year. They move to warmer climates, to find food, or a safe place to breed and raise their young. Migrations can cover thousands of miles. Many polar seabirds migrate enormous distances, but the Arctic tern makes the longest journey of all creatures. Each year, it travels from the top to the bottom of the globe and back again— a journey of 9,300 miles (15,000 km). Whales mate and give birth in warm seas, but they migrate to polar seas to eat the huge amounts of krill they need. Marine turtles can spend more than a year building up the fat reserves they will need when they leave their feeding grounds. They journey across vast oceans to certain regions where they mate and lay their eggs. But how do marine turtles navigate over the open ocean with such accuracy? There is much about animal migration that continues to baffle scientists.

BABY TURTLES
These turtles make an instinctive dash for the sea after hatching in the sand. But once in the sea, they are easy targets for predators, such as sharks. Most do not survive.

48

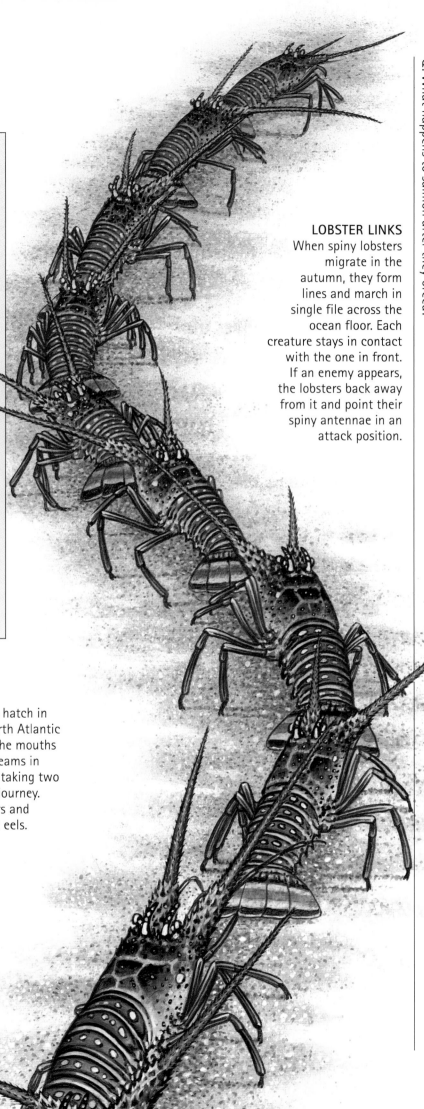

THE LIFE CYCLE OF A SALMON

Salmon lay their eggs in freshwater rivers and streams. Young salmon, called alevin, hatch in gravel on the river bed and remain there for several weeks. Then they begin to swim downstream to the salty ocean, where they will feed on fish, squid and krill. This migration usually takes place at night to avoid predators. Salmon spend up to four years at sea before returning to breed in the river in which they were hatched. Some adult salmon will travel thousands of miles to reach these rivers. After breeding, the salmon die.

SALMON EGGS
Salmon hide their large yolky eggs in the gravel of river beds to keep them safe from predators. Young salmon feed on their yolk sac.

SWIMMING UPSTREAM
Leaping sockeye salmon fight their way back up the Adams River, Canada, to their home spawning grounds.

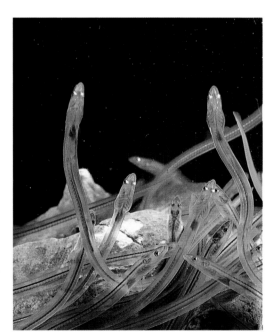

ON THE MOVE
The larvae of European eels hatch in the Sargasso Sea, in the north Atlantic Ocean. Then they swim to the mouths of freshwater rivers and streams in North America and Europe, taking two to three years to make the journey. Here they change into elvers and gradually mature into adult eels.

LOBSTER LINKS
When spiny lobsters migrate in the autumn, they form lines and march in single file across the ocean floor. Each creature stays in contact with the one in front. If an enemy appears, the lobsters back away from it and point their spiny antennae in an attack position.

Food from the Sea

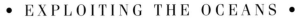

People have gathered food from the sea for thousands of years. Fish and shellfish are rich in protein and essential nutrients, and people in many countries include great amounts of fish in their diet. There are different ways of taking food from the sea: fishing with a hook, line and sinker; placing baskets and pots in the sea to catch crabs, lobsters akd crayfish; setting up fish farms, where huge quantities of fish, mollusks and crustaceans are produced each year; and using fishing ships with modern equipment and techniques. These large vessels take millions of tons of fish, such as herring, tuna, cod and mackerel, from the sea every year to provide food for humans, and to turn into fish oil, animal feed and fertilizers. They find most of their catch in the waters that are close to the coast, where fish flock to find food.

Crab

TO CATCH A TUNA
Tuna are not easy to catch. They are very large and heavy, and it can take four men to land a tuna such as this on the deck of a boat. Some tuna will trail a fishing boat for a long time and then steal the bait without being caught.

A CHOICE MENU
There is an enormous variety of food from the sea: fish, octopuses, squid, eels, shrimp and many more are caught and sold to people all over the world.

FARMING OYSTERS
Many oyster farms are located in waters that are rich with microscopic algae, the natural food of oysters. The oysters are grown in trays or on sticks, and are usually harvested from 18 months to 3 years old.

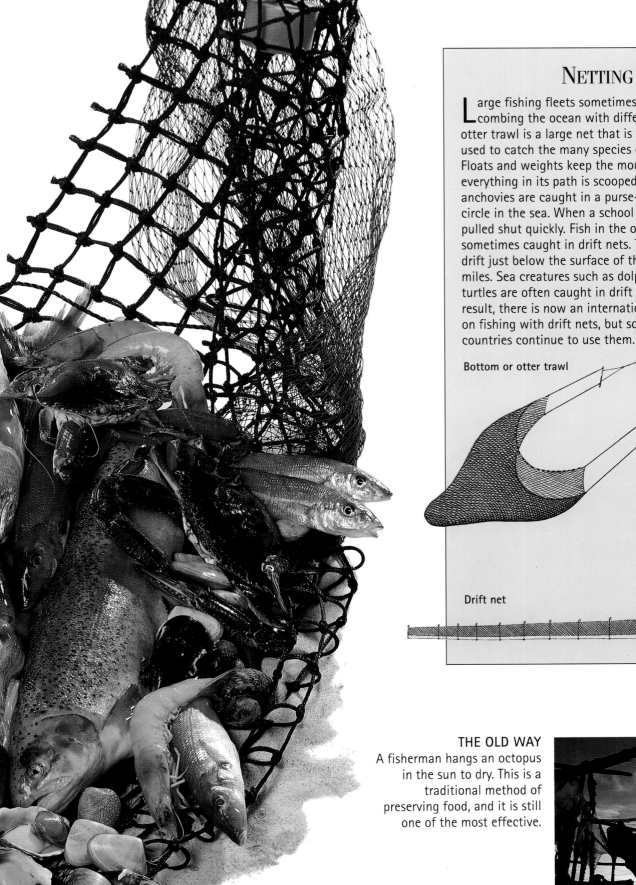

NETTING THE CATCH

Large fishing fleets sometimes spend several months at sea, combing the ocean with different types of nets. A bottom or otter trawl is a large net that is towed behind a fishing boat and used to catch the many species of fish that live on the sea bed. Floats and weights keep the mouth of the trawl open so that everything in its path is scooped up. Species of fish such as anchovies are caught in a purse-seine net, which forms a large circle in the sea. When a school of fish swims into the net, it is pulled shut quickly. Fish in the open seas, such as tuna, are sometimes caught in drift nets. These are held up by floats and drift just below the surface of the water for many miles. Sea creatures such as dolphins and sea turtles are often caught in drift nets. As a result, there is now an international ban on fishing with drift nets, but some countries continue to use them.

Bottom or otter trawl

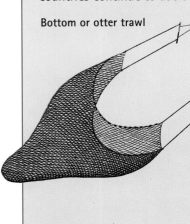

Purse seine

Drift net

THE OLD WAY
A fisherman hangs an octopus in the sun to dry. This is a traditional method of preserving food, and it is still one of the most effective.

DID YOU KNOW?
In Japan, China and other parts of Asia, cormorants are sometimes used to dive for fish. Fishermen attach a line to the birds' bodies so that they can pull them back to the boat. A ring or cord around the birds' necks stops them from swallowing the fish they catch in their mouths.

Discover more in Ocean Meadows

51

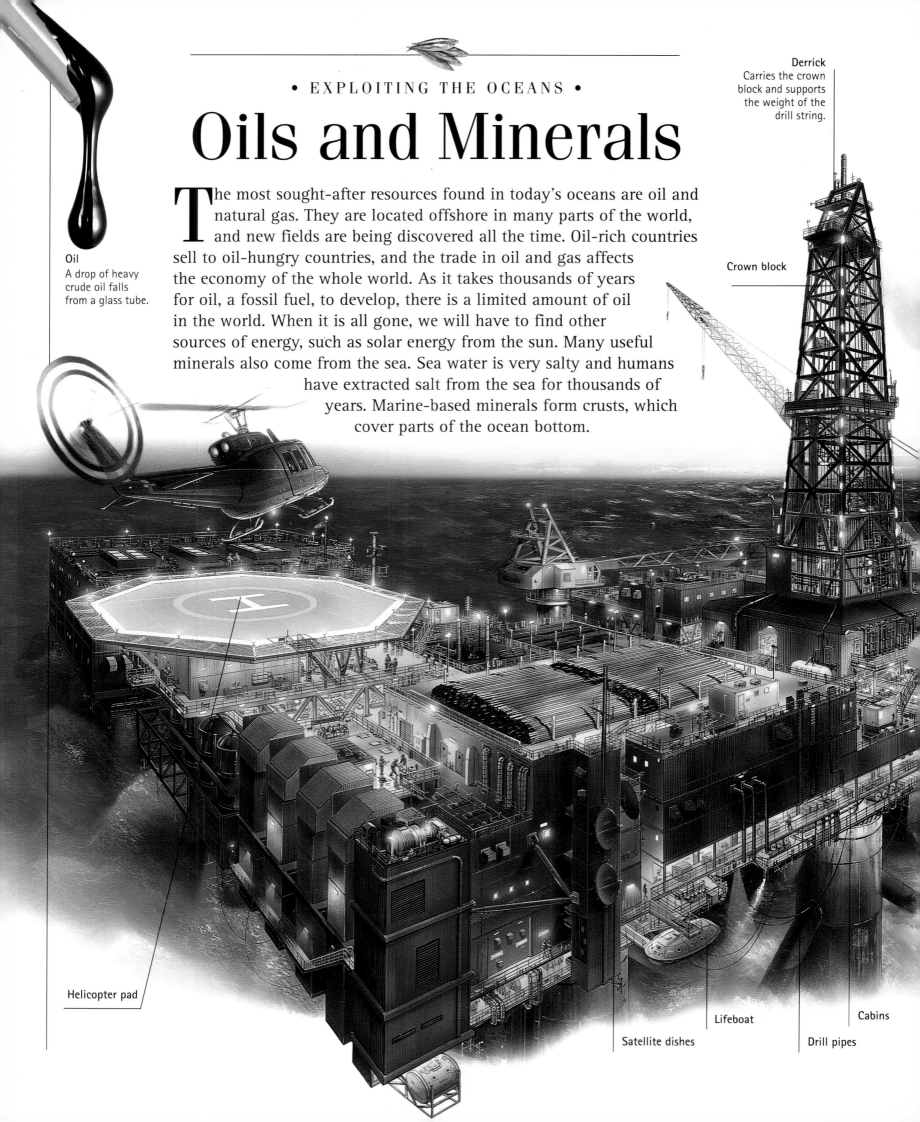

Oils and Minerals

The most sought-after resources found in today's oceans are oil and natural gas. They are located offshore in many parts of the world, and new fields are being discovered all the time. Oil-rich countries sell to oil-hungry countries, and the trade in oil and gas affects the economy of the whole world. As it takes thousands of years for oil, a fossil fuel, to develop, there is a limited amount of oil in the world. When it is all gone, we will have to find other sources of energy, such as solar energy from the sun. Many useful minerals also come from the sea. Sea water is very salty and humans have extracted salt from the sea for thousands of years. Marine-based minerals form crusts, which cover parts of the ocean bottom.

Oil
A drop of heavy crude oil falls from a glass tube.

Derrick
Carries the crown block and supports the weight of the drill string.

Crown block

Helicopter pad

Lifeboat

Satellite dishes

Drill pipes

Cabins

WHAT IS OIL?

Oil was formed when dead plants and animals sank to the bottom of the ocean. The dead matter was buried under piles of mud and sand, which turned into rock after millions of years. The decaying matter was squashed and, as the temperature and pressure increased, it collected in the sedimentary rock as droplets of oil held between the rock grains— just like a sponge holds water.

MINING FOR MANGANESE

Manganese is a hard, brittle metal element. It is used to make alloys, such as steel, harder and stronger. Manganese nodules are found on parts of the ocean floor. The ones shown here were dredged from the Blake Plateau in the North Atlantic Ocean, 1,378 ft (420 m) below the surface. Manganese nodules form in places where sediment builds up slowly. As each new layer of metal is added, the nodules grow bigger, sometimes joining together with other nodules. Most nodules look like small black potatoes and grow at the rate of a few millimeters every million years. Some of the world's mining companies have located rich deposits of deep-sea manganese nodules. However, mining manganese is an extremely expensive process. First, the nodules must be dredged, often in very deep waters, and transported back to shore. Then, they must be treated with chemicals to extract the manganese. At the moment, this is all too costly and the manganese nodules on the ocean floors remain largely untouched.

Revolving crane

Flare

Well heads
Transport oil and gas to the platform.

Processing equipment

DRILLING DEEP

Several oil wells extend at different angles through the layers of strata until they reach a pocket of oil.

Water level
The water level of the ocean rises and falls with the tides.

Shales and porous rocks
Water passes through the widely spaced rock grains of shale, sandstone and limestone.

Impermeable layer
A layer of dense rock forms a lid on top of the layer of oil or gas.

An oil and water mix
Oil, water and gas form pockets in the grains of porous rocks. Small amounts of oil and water mix together here.

Non-porous rocks
This layer, which is often granite, stops the oil from escaping downwards.

DRILLING FOR GOLD

An oil platform is like a huge steel and concrete hotel in the middle of the ocean. Several hundred workers can live there for weeks at a time. Most platforms stay in position for about 25 years, although one rig has survived for 60 years. Every day, these platforms pump millions of barrels of oil or "black gold," a name often given to this sticky, black, expensive liquid.

Lifeboat

CHECKING THE FOUNDATIONS

Divers must make routine checks of all the pipes and cables under an oil rig. Pounding seas constantly batter the rig and can eventually wear away or dislodge even the strongest metal framework.

The Perils of Pollution

Human and industrial waste has been dumped in the sea for years. People once believed that sea water could kill any lurking germs. But scientists have now discovered that sewage pumped into the sea can spread terrible diseases, such as cholera, typhus and hepatitis. If polluting material enters the food chain, it can become more and more dangerous as one creature eats another. Humans are at the end of the food chain and they can suffer the worst effects of all. In the 1950s, many people in Japan died or became paralyzed after eating fish that was contaminated with mercury from a local factory. The United Nations began to take marine pollution seriously in the 1970s, but by this time, parts of some seas were already dying. Today, oceans are still polluted by oil spills, chemicals and human waste.

A GIANT GARBAGE CAN
Humans throw all kinds of litter into the sea, but this garbage never goes away.

A HAZARDOUS LIFE
This seal is entangled in a carelessly discarded fishing line. Any material thrown into the sea is potentially harmful to sea creatures. Nets, plastic balloons and the ring openers of soft-drink cans kill many sea mammals, sea birds and fish.

STRANGE BUT TRUE
This hermit crab was found with a very unnatural shell— a plastic bucket in which it is now trapped.

SPILLING OIL

Oil
pick-up
point

Road

Oil spill

Boom

Harbour
entrance

Wind direction

When an oil tanker spills its liquid cargo into the sea, floating booms are erected. They try to trap the oil and stop it from polluting the shoreline. The trapped oil is sucked up and stored somewhere safe. But it is not always possible to stop the oil from spreading. These workers are hosing the rocky coastline of Alaska in the huge clean-up operation that followed the *Exxon Valdez* oil spill.

BLUE-GREEN ALGAE
Clouds of marine algae, which grow when water is polluted, float near the surface of the Sea of Cortez. The algae shade the sea bottom and stop the rich seagrasses from growing. Without this source of food, fish, shellfish and worms will suffer.

THE BEGINNING
This undeveloped beach in Cyprus is already littered with trash from the ocean.

LOSING LIFE
Oil spills at sea are devastating for wildlife. When a bird's feathers are covered with oil, they are no longer waterproof. Water soaks into the unprotected feathers and the bird drowns or freezes to death.

55

The Future of the Oceans

Who owns the sea and who should look after it? How can we ensure that its vast resources, which we need for food, fuel and energy, are not used up completely? Will future generations be able to swim in clear, unpolluted water? If we want to protect the sea, we must manage it properly. All the continents in the world are surrounded by sea, so people from all countries must cooperate to preserve it. Important steps, such as establishing marine parks to protect endangered environments and species, have already been taken. Many nations have signed agreements to limit activities such as drift-net fishing, which can harm sea animals. But overfishing and pollution continue to threaten the sea. There is much to do to guarantee its future.

BEACHED!
Whales that swim too close to the shore may become stranded. They need water to support their bodies— without it they cannot breathe and will die. Volunteers work hard to keep this whale's skin wet until it can be floated out to sea on the high tide.

RESPECTING NATURE
A sea bird nesting on land seems unperturbed by such close inspection. We need to protect the natural environment so that we can continue to enjoy seeing animals in their natural world.

CROWN-OF-THORNS
The crown-of-thorns starfish stays hidden during the day and comes out at night to feed on the coral that surrounds it. It eats the coral tissue and leaves nothing but a skeleton behind it. This starfish has caused great damage to reefs in the Indo-Pacific area during the last twenty years.

MANAGING THE OCEANS
The oceans link all the countries of the world. Different nations can manage the oceans by:

• Creating marine parks to protect marine life.

• Working out who owns particular areas of the sea and whose responsibility it is to look after it. Countries own and manage all living and non-living resources for 200 nautical miles from their low-water line. The rest of the oceans are international zones and are not controlled by any one nation.

• Placing bans or limits on some forms of drag-net fishing and whaling, both of which kill sea creatures senselessly.

• Trying to stop or control the amount and type of pollution that is pumped into the sea.

• Monitoring the seaworthiness and age of all vessels allowed to operate on the sea.

• Making sure that nuclear-powered vessels and oil tankers are not allowed anywhere near national parks, populated areas or any other sensitive areas close to the coasts.

• Ensuring that destructive animals such as the crown-of-thorns starfish are controlled and not allowed to damage heritage areas such as Australia's Great Barrier Reef.

SELLING SEA SHELLS
Many people collect shells for their unusual shapes and colors. But these shells are the homes of many seashore animals. Their habitat is destroyed when people remove the shells from the seashore.

COMMUNITY CARE
A responsible hiker carries his trash home with him. If people leave garbage at a camping site, especially one near a river, it can eventually pollute the ocean.

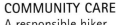

Conserving the Oceans

Each year there are 90 million more people on Earth to feed. Because the biggest increase in population is in coastal areas, more seafood is needed each year to feed the world. Sadly, most of the traditional fisheries of the oceans have either reached the limit of safe fishing or are already past that point and are now being overfished. If we want to keep the great ocean fisheries at their most productive, we must stop polluting them and also be more moderate in the numbers of fish we catch. This much-needed increase in the numbers of fish and shellfish can only happen in clean, unpolluted waters. Numbers can be further increased by opening new fisheries and by setting up fish farms in coastal lagoons and ponds, or within big nets in shallow water.

MARINE PARKS

Coral reefs are breaking down all over the world from the effects of pollution and overfishing. To prevent this, most tropical countries are creating marine parks to help protect coral areas from further damage. Tourists can still enjoy the reefs and their fishes at these parks. The largest of these sanctuaries is the Great Barrier Reef Marine Park. It extends for 1,240 miles (2,000 km) along the coast of northeastern Australia.

African Tilapia
Fish farming is a huge and growing industry in southeast Asia. Many local species are used, but African tilapias are very popular. Scientists have made genetic changes to the tilapia to increase dramatically the growth rate of this fish and to allow a greater number of fish crops per year.

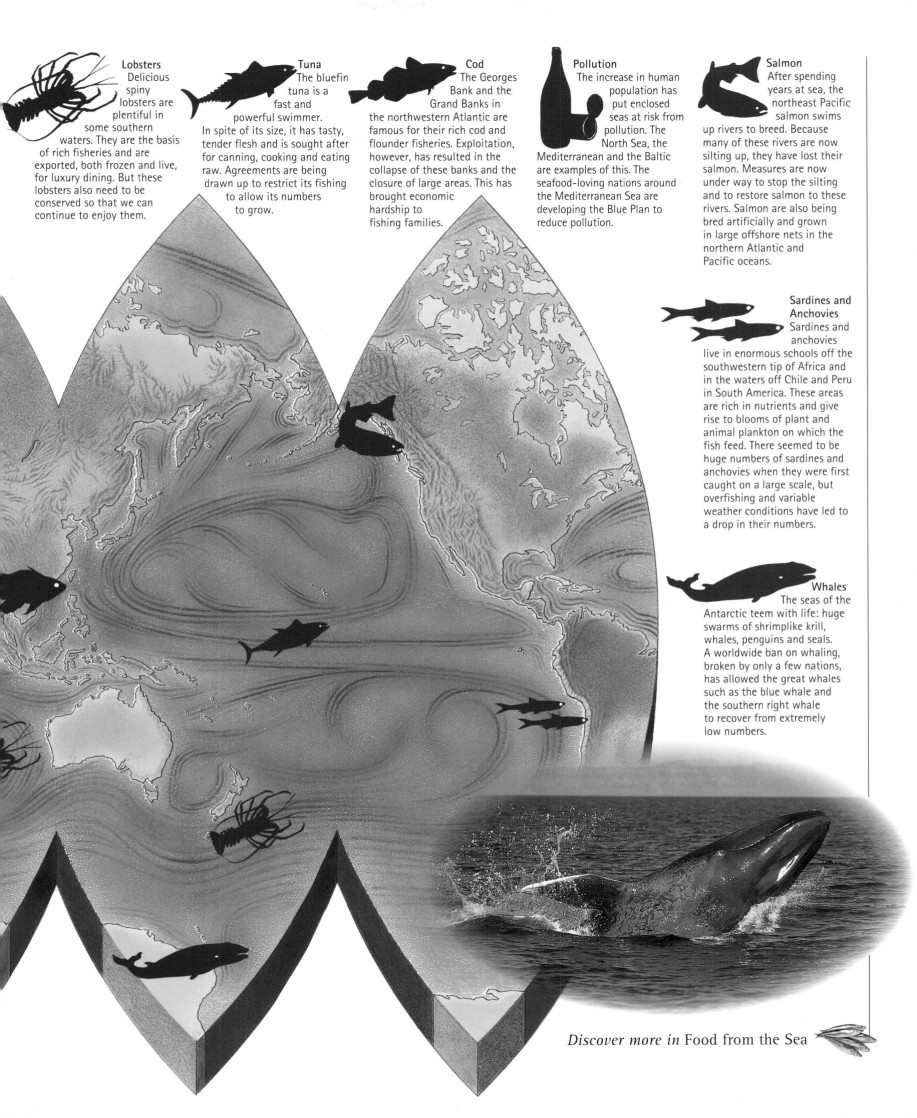

Lobsters
Delicious spiny lobsters are plentiful in some southern waters. They are the basis of rich fisheries and are exported, both frozen and live, for luxury dining. But these lobsters also need to be conserved so that we can continue to enjoy them.

Tuna
The bluefin tuna is a fast and powerful swimmer. In spite of its size, it has tasty, tender flesh and is sought after for canning, cooking and eating raw. Agreements are being drawn up to restrict its fishing to allow its numbers to grow.

Cod
The Georges Bank and the Grand Banks in the northwestern Atlantic are famous for their rich cod and flounder fisheries. Exploitation, however, has resulted in the collapse of these banks and the closure of large areas. This has brought economic hardship to fishing families.

Pollution
The increase in human population has put enclosed seas at risk from pollution. The North Sea, the Mediterranean and the Baltic are examples of this. The seafood-loving nations around the Mediterranean Sea are developing the Blue Plan to reduce pollution.

Salmon
After spending years at sea, the northeast Pacific salmon swims up rivers to breed. Because many of these rivers are now silting up, they have lost their salmon. Measures are now under way to stop the silting and to restore salmon to these rivers. Salmon are also being bred artificially and grown in large offshore nets in the northern Atlantic and Pacific oceans.

Sardines and Anchovies
Sardines and anchovies live in enormous schools off the southwestern tip of Africa and in the waters off Chile and Peru in South America. These areas are rich in nutrients and give rise to blooms of plant and animal plankton on which the fish feed. There seemed to be huge numbers of sardines and anchovies when they were first caught on a large scale, but overfishing and variable weather conditions have led to a drop in their numbers.

Whales
The seas of the Antarctic teem with life: huge swarms of shrimplike krill, whales, penguins and seals. A worldwide ban on whaling, broken by only a few nations, has allowed the great whales such as the blue whale and the southern right whale to recover from extremely low numbers.

Discover more in Food from the Sea

Ocean Facts

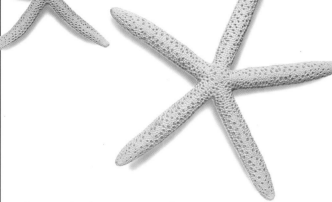

Water makes up two-thirds of the surface of the Earth. The Southern Hemisphere is particularly wet, with four times as much water as land. With the help of technology, we are learning how the oceans were formed, how they are changing, how they are responsible for our weather and how important they are to plant and animal life.

What is the largest ocean?

The Pacific Ocean covers 65 million square miles (166 million square km) and makes up 32 per cent of the Earth's surface. It is the world's largest and deepest ocean. On average, its sea floor is 13,737 ft (4,188 m) below sea level.

What is the deepest part of the deepest ocean?

The deepest part is the Mariana Trench near the Philippines in the Pacific Ocean. It is 35,620 ft (10,860 m) below sea level. If you turned Mount Everest, the world's highest mountain, upside down in the trench, it would sink more than 1 mile (2 km) into the sea before touching the bottom.

How do fish survive in the freezing temperature of the polar regions?

As sea water freezes sooner than the blood of fish, a number of Arctic and Antarctic fish have developed an organic anti-freeze mechanism to survive in the cold waters.

Why is the sea salty?

The sea gets its salt from rocks on the sea bed and from rivers that feed into it. As the sea is evaporated by the sun, the salt level builds up.

Which oceans cover the Earth?

The Pacific, Atlantic, Indian, Southern and Arctic oceans are the five oceans that cover the Earth.

How much water do the oceans hold?

The oceans hold 48 billion cubic ft (1,358 cubic decimeters) of water.

What does the word "ocean" mean?

The word ocean comes from the Greek word "okeanos," which means river. The early Greeks thought that a river encircled the Earth.

Which is the strongest ocean current?

The Gulf Stream carries about 30 billion gallons (135 billion liters) of water every second. This is 6.5 times as much water as all the rivers in the world.

Does the ocean ever overflow?

Rain, melting ice and river water pour continually into the ocean. But the ocean never overflows because this water is always on the move. It is evaporated by the sun and turned into water vapor. The vapor then falls as rain or snow, most of which ends up back in the ocean. This is usually turned back into vapor and the whole cycle starts once again.

How did the Dead Sea get its name?
This sea is so salty that nothing can live in its water.

What is the difference between an ocean and a sea?
Seas are shallower and smaller than oceans and are partly surrounded by land.

Which sea is growing wider by 0.4 in (1 cm) each year?
The Red Sea is growing by this amount every year as the Earth's lithospheric plates move apart and the sea floor spreads.

How many kinds of shark live in the oceans?
Scientists know of 350 species of shark, most of them harmless.

What percentage of the Netherlands lies below sea level?
More than 33 per cent of the Netherlands is below sea level. Windmills control the amount of water that reaches the fields lying below the sea's surface.

If no more water was added to the oceans and evaporation continued normally, how long would it take for the oceans to dry up?
If this happened, it would take 3,000 years.

How much of the sea bed is still unexplored?
Ninety-eight per cent of the sea bed is still to be explored, but as advances in underwater technology continue, more exploration will take place.

Which is the saltiest sea on Earth?
The salt content of sea water is usually about 3.5 per cent. The Dead Sea, however, contains more than 24 per cent— nearly eight times as much!

What is the biggest fish in the ocean?
The whale shark is the largest fish. It grows up to 49 ft (15 m) in length.

How much of an iceberg do you actually see?
Nine-tenths of an iceberg is hidden under the water so you can only see one-tenth.

What is the oldest form of marine life still found in the oceans?
A form of blue-green algae has existed for some billions of years. Sharks are some of the oldest back-boned animals in the sea.

Where is the world's highest inland sea?
Lake Titicaca between Peru and Bolivia is the highest inland sea. Its surface is 12,503 ft (3,812 m) above sea level.

Which sea is the most polluted in the world?
The Mediterranean is the world's most polluted sea. More than 421 billion tons (430 billion tonnes) of pollution are poured into it each year.

Why is the sea blue?
The light that strikes the sea is either absorbed or broken up and scattered back to the surface. Blue and green wavelengths of light are scattered more than red and yellow ones, and this gives the sea its blue or green appearance.

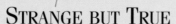

STRANGE BUT TRUE
Some fish can change sex easily. The black-and-gold angelfish of the South Pacific live in groups of one male and up to seven females. If the male dies, the largest female turns into a male within a week or two.

Glossary

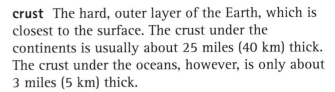

Scallop shells

Queen angelfish

Submersible

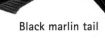

Emperor penguins

Black marlin tail

abyssal plain A vast, flat, barren area under the sea that spreads from the mid-oceanic ridge to where the continents begin.

alevin The young of salmon, which hatch in gravel on river beds.

algae The simplest forms of plant life.

Antarctic The extremely cold region at the South Pole, which is south of the Antarctic Circle.

Arctic The very cold region at the North Pole, which is north of the Arctic Circle.

basin A large, cup-shaped dent in the sea floor.

bathysphere A sphere-shaped diving vessel used by scientists to study deep-sea life.

bathythermograph A scientific instrument used to measure underwater temperatures.

Beaufort Scale This is used to indicate the strength of the wind at sea. It was named after Francis Beaufort, a British admiral.

bioluminescence The production of light by living organisms, such as the bacteria that live on some deep-sea fish.

black smokers Mineral chimneys on the ocean floor. They spurt black smoke and hot water rich in sulphur, which some deep-sea dwellers use to make food.

blowhole The nostril (can be one or two) on top of a whale's head through which it breathes.

camouflage The ability of an animal to blend in with its natural surroundings to avoid predators or to catch food.

cartographer A person who is specially trained to draw maps.

continental shelf A flat, projecting extension of land submerged beneath a shallow sea.

continental slope The gently sloping, submerged land near the coast that forms the side of an ocean basin.

coral polyp A tube-shaped animal with a soft body and a circle of tentacles at the top. More than 400 species of coral live in colonies in the oceans.

coral reef A structure that is made from the skeletons of soft-bodied coral animals or polyps, and is found in warm waters.

crust The hard, outer layer of the Earth, which is closest to the surface. The crust under the continents is usually about 25 miles (40 km) thick. The crust under the oceans, however, is only about 3 miles (5 km) thick.

crustacean An animal such as a lobster, crab or prawn that has a hard skeleton on the outside of its body.

dorsal fin A fin on the back of some fish. It helps the fish keep its balance as it moves through the water.

estuary The mouth of a river where its currents meet the ocean's tides.

fisher scoop A scientific instrument used for scooping up sand and mud samples from the sea bed. Oceanographers analyze the specimens to help them understand how the underwater landscape was formed.

fossil fuel A fuel such as oil, coal and natural gas, which has been formed from plant or animal remains and is embedded deep within the Earth. Fossil fuels take millions of years to form.

gill The organ that sea-living creatures such as fish use for breathing.

guyot An underwater volcano with a flat top.

gyre One of the five giant loops of moving water or currents, which are driven by the wind. They circle in a clockwise direction in the Northern Hemisphere, where there are two gyres, and in a counterclockwise direction in the Southern Hemisphere, where there are three gyres.

iceberg A large, floating chunk of ice, broken off from a glacier and carried out to sea.

invertebrate An animal without a backbone.

krill A shrimp-like crustacean that lives in large numbers in Arctic waters.

lithospheric plates The main rigid, outer surfaces of the Earth, which are formed from the upper part of the Earth's mantle and the crust.

marine park An area of the ocean set aside as a reserve to protect endangered species and to preserve the marine environment.

migration Birds, fish and many animals travel from one habitat to another at certain times of the year to find food or to give birth to their young.

mineral A material appearing in nature that is extracted by mining.

mollusk An animal, such as a snail, squid or octopus, with no backbone and a soft body that can be enclosed or partly enclosed by a shell.

mother ship A ship that provides supplies for one or more smaller vessels, such as submersibles.

navigation The science of directing the course of a ship or an aircraft.

neap tide The smallest rise and fall in tides that occurs when the sun and the moon are at right angles to the Earth.

ocean A very large stretch of water.

ocean current A huge mass of water that travels enormous distances and mixes warm water near the equator with cold water from the polar regions.

oceanic ridge A long, narrow chain of underwater mountains formed when two of the Earth's plates meet and magma wells up to the surface to form a new sea floor.

oceanic trench A long, narrow valley under the sea that contains some of the deepest points on Earth.

oceanographer A person who studies the science of the oceans.

oceanography The science of the features and the structure of the ocean.

pillow lava Lava formed when hot gases and liquid bubble up through the sea floor and harden. This lava then becomes part of a new sea bed.

plankton The tiny plant or animal organisms that drift near the surface of the water and which form an important link in the food chain.

photophores Special organs in animals, especially fish, which are able to produce light.

phytoplankton Tiny, single-celled algae that float on the surface of the sea. Seaweed and other large algae grow along the seashore and in shallow water.

predator An animal that preys on other animals for food.

sea A body of water that is partly or completely enclosed by land.

seamount A large, underwater volcanic mountain that remains under the sea or rises above it to form an island.

sediment Mineral or organic matter that contains millions of tiny animals and plants, and which settles at the bottom of the sea. The layer of sediment blanketing the sea plains may be 984–1,640 ft (300–500 m) thick.

spring tide The greatest rise and fall in tides that occurs when the sun and the moon are in line with the Earth.

submersible A small submarine that is able to reach the depths of the ocean, or to probe inside places that are too small for ordinary vessels. Submersibles are often used to explore shipwrecks.

tentacle A slender, flexible feeler that enables an animal with no backbone to touch things.

tide The repeating rise and fall of the Earth's seas, caused by the pull of the moon and sun on the water.

tropical cyclone An enormous mass of rapidly whirling air, formed as moist, sun-heated air starts to rise and colder air takes its place. A tropical cyclone is sometimes called a hurricane or a typhoon.

tsunami A gigantic, often destructive, sea wave which is triggered by an underwater earthquake or volcano.

venom A poisonous fluid that is transmitted by a bite or a sting.

volcanoes Underwater volcanoes are called seamounts. Some may break the surface of the ocean and form volcanic islands.

waterspout A whirling column of air that hangs down from the bottom of some clouds. It occurs when warm, moist, rising air meets cold, dry air. Waterspouts are similiar to tornadoes and can be destructive.

whirlpool A whirling, circular movement of water created when the tide turns and the opposing currents meet.

zooplankton Tiny plant-eating sea creatures that eat phytoplankton and which are in turn eaten by small meat-eating creatures.

Giant squid

Nautilus shell

Paper nautilus eggs

Spanish coins

Blue-swimmer crab

Index

Picture Credits

(t=top, b=bottom, l=left, r=right, c=center, i=icon, F=front,
C=cover, B=back, Bg=background)
Ad-Libitum, 5b,13cr, 42tl, 50i, 50-51, 50bl, 50cl, 50tl, 52i, 54i, 56i, 57t, 57cℰtr, 58i, 59i, 60c, 60t, 62t, 63b, 63tc (S. Bowey). Auscape, 58bl (K. Deacon) 48bl, 57tl (J.P. Ferrero) 59br (F. Gohier) 17cl (C. A. Henley) 18bc, 21tl, 63c (D. Parer ℰ E. Parer-Cook) 23cl (M. Tinsley) 20-21 (A. Ziebell). Austral International, 40cl (R. Parry/Rex Features). Australian Museum, 4c, 4t, 5c, 6i, 8i, 10i, 12i, 14i, 16i, 18i, 20i, 22i, 24i, 26i, 28i, 30i, 31i, 32i, 44i, 46i, 48i, 51i (H. Pinelli). Australian National Maritime Collection, 38br (S. Bowey/Ad-Libitum). Australian Picture Library, 38cr, (Bettmann Archive/UPI) 19cr (Volvox) 61r (L. Meier) 61bl (Lℰl. Meier). Esther Beaton, 54tr, 55bc, 55l, 55tl. Biofotos, 49bl (H. Angel) 62tc (I. Took). Bruce Coleman Ltd, 54bl (A. Compost) 24br (F. J. Erize) 27bl (I. Everson) 49c (J. Foott) 21br, 21bcl (CℰtℰS. Hood) 20-21b, 21tr (J. Murray) 24c, 62bc (H. Reinhard)16-17cr,17t (F. Sauer) 20tl (N. Sefton) 15cl (K. Taylor) 54l (J. Topham) 20bc (B. Wood). James Cook University, 9 (D. Johnson). Kevin Deacon, 23tl (Dive 2000) DJC ℰ Associates, 57br (D. J. Cox). Mary Evans Picture Library,*11tl (Photo Researchers Inc) 31cl, 38ttc, 44tl, 45tr, 46tl, 47br. The Granger Collection, 34i, 35i, 38i, 40i, 42i, 43i, 45br, 47b. Greenpeace, 55br (Beltra) 55bl (Midgley). Richard Herrmann, 17b, 17br. Ifremer, 33r. Images Unlimited Inc, 40tr (A. Giddings) 8tl (C. Nicklin). Minden Pictures,
35br (J. Brandenberg) 51br, 54-55, 56, 57cl (F. Lanting) 16cl (F. Nicklin). National Maritime Museum Greenwich, 34bc, 34bl, 39tl. NHPA 28tl (Agence Nature) 45bc, 49tl (G. I. Bernard) 58cl (B. Jones ℰ M. Shimlock) 21cr (B. Wood). Oxford Scientific Films, 17bc (A. Atkinson) 22-23b (G. I. Bernard) 21bc (L. Gould) 16t, 22cl, 23cr (H. Hall) 20t (M. Hall) 24cl (B. Osborne) 26br, 28tr (P. Parks) 22bl (D. Shale) 26bl, 26cr (H. Taylor Abipp) 23tr (K. Westerskov). The Photo Library, Sydney, 52tl (H. Frieder Michler/SPL) 47r (D. Hardy/SPL) 27cr (NASA/SPL) 12tl (J. Sanford/SPL) 6cr, 11bl, 11cl (SPL) 55cr (V. Vick). Photo Researchers Inc, 8bl (J. R. Factor) 6br (NASA/SPL) 53r (G. Whiteley). Planet Earth Pictures, 20c (G. Bell) 55c (M. Conlin) 28r, 29cr, 29bcr, 29tl, 31c, 31tr (P. David) 8br (R. Hessler) 54l (C. Howes) 23br (A. Kerstitch)22t, 29c (K. Lucas) 16t (J. Lythgoe) 29tcr (L. Madin) 25bl (R. Matthews) 40tl, 62c (D. Perrine) 24tr (P. Sayers) 8c (F. Schulke) 20bl, 22cr (P. Scoones) 57bl (W. Williams). Queensland Museum, 36t, 36tl (G. Cranitch). Jeffrey L. Rotman, 1, 35tl, 35tr, 50tr, 63bc. Science Museum, London, 34l (Science ℰ Society Picture Library). Scripps Institution of Oceanography, University of California, San Diego, 43tr. Marty Snyderman, 53bl. State Library of New South Wales, Image Library, 34bl, 39b, 39br, 39cr, 39r, 39tr. Stock Photos, 60-61 (Bill Bachman). Survival Anglia, 15tr (J. Foott). Woods Hole Oceanographic Institution, 42br, 43tl. Norbert Wu, 23c, 29bc, 29br, 29tr, 55r.

Photo Manipulation

Richard Wilson Studios, 16-17, 20-21, 54-55, 56-57.

Illustration Credits

Graham Back, 22-23. Greg Bridges, 46-47. Rod Burchett, 55tr. Simone End, 4bl, 4-5tc, 31bc, 57bc, 63tr. Christer Eriksson, 2-3, 4-5bc, 6tl, 12-13, 16-17, 24-25, 44-45. Mike Golding, 18bl, 19br. Mike Gorman, 58-59. Richard Hook, 34/39. David Kirshner, 5br, 15tr, 18-19bc, 26br, 28bl, 28br, 29bl, 30-31, 62bl. Robyn Latimer, 58-59. Alex Lavroff, 11br, 19br, 40bl. Colin Newman, 5tr, 14-15. Oliver Rennert, 6-7, 6bl, 8-9, 40-41. Ken Rinkel, 41r. Trevor Ruth, 4tl, 10-11, 11tr, 32-33, 48-49. Rod Scott, 18-19, 26-27. Steve Seymour, 42-43, 52-53. Ray Sim, 12bl, 13tl, 51tr. Kevin Stead, 35/38. Rod Westblade, endpapers.

Cover Credits

Ad-Libitum, BCtl, FCtr (S. Bowey). Auscape, FCcr, Bg (L. Newman ℰ A. Flowers). Biofotos, FCtl (I. Took). Bruce Coleman Ltd, FCbcl, FCbr (C. ℰ S. Hood) FCbl, FCtcr (J. Murray). Mike Golding, FCcl. NHPA, FCbcr (B. Wood). Oxford Scientific Films, FCbc (L. Gould). Richard Wilson Studios, FCb.